The Jesus Prescription for a Healthy Life

Leonard Sweet

Abingdon Press
Nashville

THE JESUS PRESCRIPTION FOR A HEALTHY LIFE

Copyright © 1996 by Abingdon Press

This book is printed on recycled, acid-free paper.

Library of Congress Cataloging-in-Publication Data

Sweet, Leonard I.
    The Jesus prescription for a healthy life / Leonard Sweet.
      p.   cm.
    Includes bibliographical references.
    ISBN 0-687-01491-3 (pbk. : alk. paper)
    1. Health—Religious aspects—Christianity. 2. Stress (Psychology)—Religious aspects—Christianity. I. Title.
BT732.S934   1996
248.8′6—dc20
                                             96-1314
                                           CIP

99 00 01 02 03 04 05—10 9 8 7 6 5

MANUFACTURED IN THE UNITED STATES OF AMERICA

For Justin

That Jesus May Be Not a Word But a Way of Life

We are a downright uptight people.

"We are fast becoming a nation of the quick, or the dead-tired" announces a *Newsweek* cover article on America's frazzled, frenzied state. A Louis Harris poll reports that 86 percent of Americans report chronic stress, while 60 percent do nothing about stress but carry it around. One out of four of us feels "stressed and stretched into exhaustion."[1] We are a nation of worriers, a people who are "pushed—and pushing—too hard." We stew and fret—about stress and anxiety.

We compete to be on the best-stressed list. We are a nation of overweights overcoming being overwhelmed and overworked. The International Labor Organization, an arm of the United Nations, calls job stress "the twentieth century disease." Estimating the cost of job stress in USAmerica alone at $200 billion annually, stress-related injuries on the job have risen dramatically—from 5 percent of all occupational disease claims in 1980 to 15 percent a decade later. Another recent study found that 38 percent of Americans "always feel rushed." Job stress has almost become a badge of honor. Even though librarians come in dead-last of all professions treated for job-related stress, they still have their guide to overcoming the stress of librarianship: *Stress and Burnout in Library Service* (1991).

Physician Robert Anderson, who specializes in stress-related illnesses, testifies that whereas he once attributed to stress 30 to 40 percent of the problems presented by patients, he now thinks stress may be implicated in 90 percent of ailments.[2]

Fatigue is already among the top five reasons people call their doctors. Of the top twenty prescription drugs, eleven are for treatment of high blood pressure or ulcers—stress disorders.

Increasingly, more people are spending less time cooking than brushing their teeth.[3] Juliet B. Schor's *The Overworked American* documents why there are so many "famous flame-outs" and breakdowns in recent years: She claims (not without skepticism) that full-time employees in 1987 worked 163 more hours than in 1969.[4] Another researcher found that USAmerican workers put in 5 percent more hours a week than workers in Europe.

But the "stressed-out" phenomenon is global. The Japanese even have a name for the most severe form of this syndrome: *karaoshi,* or death from overwork, which takes a toll of thirty thousand Japanese workers every year. No wonder time is now more prized than money; people would rather spend money for something than spend time for it.

The best way to get on the best-stressed list? Be a working mom! More than air-traffic controllers, more than emergency room physicians, more than inner-city teachers— working moms tally more points on the stress-o-meter than virtually anyone else. A woman living in the mideighties with school-age children spent eleven hours per week simply driving around.

It's not just IBMs and PTAs that cause this epidemic of stress. Our churches and synagogues are major contributors. The church has turned Jesus' promise of downtime and relaxation "Come unto me and I will give you **REST**" on its head "Come unto me and I will give you **WORK**." The religious establishment of Jesus' day was little different, causing him to exclaim at one point "What stress I am under!" (Luke 12:50).

One of Jesus' methods for dealing with stress was elaborated in this principle: "If your right eye causes your downfall, tear it out" (Matt. 18:9 REB). In other

> ## *Christ the Wholemaker.*
>
> *Ricarda Huch, German poet, essayist, and novelist*

words, want to eliminate stress? Stop doing the things that cause it.

What causes a high-stress life? This entire book can be summarized in what I am calling "The Ten Commandments of Stress" or, "How to Be a Stressed-Out, Unhappy Person Most of the Time."

1. Thou shalt wear a grim expression at all times, and thou shalt hold thy body in a stiff and rigid posture, and exercise thy muscles as little as possible.
2. Thou shalt never get too close to anybody for any reason.
3. Thou shalt stuff and store all of thy feelings in thy gut.
4. Thou shalt put aside play, and shalt inflict upon others that which was once inflicted on thyself.
5. Thou shalt remain logical and analytical whenever possible.
6. Thou shalt go to as many "all-you-can-eat" buffets as thou canst.
7. Thou shalt not party.
8. Thou shalt not take a vacation.
9. Thou shalt expect the worst in all situations, blame and shame everyone around thyself for everything, and dwell on the feebleness, faults, and fears of others.
10. Thou shalt be in control at all times, no matter what.[5]

This book is a ten-step biblical guide on how to crack the code of healthy living. It is based on the life and work of Jesus of Nazareth, who himself jumped off the treadmill at thirty years of age for a spiritual calling and a health ministry. If there is one thing about Jesus on which historians are now agreed, it is that he was a healer.[6] His power flowed from a superabundance of health.[7] In criticizing old pictures of Jesus, especially Sallman's *Head of Christ*, naturalist Alan Devoe spoke of how "There was ever the quality about him of a huge healthiness, a strength and a simplicity."[8]

Jesus' teachings are a prescribed health regimen. The Sermon on the Mount is the world's best prescription for a healthy lifestyle.[9]

Jesus provides his followers a different model for discipleship than "growth." It is a "health" model of discipleship. The "church growth" movement could profit from some theological hygiene. The promise of the Gospels is not "growth." The promise is health—a healthy relationship with God, and a healthy lifestyle of wholeness, where spirit, mind, and body function synergistically. Health issues are just as much spiritual as physical and intellectual. New disorders debut daily that testify to the spiritual costs of postmodernity's unhealthy lifestyles: attention deficit disorders, eating disorders, desire disorders (compulsive sex or fear of sex), addictive disorders, and so on.

[Jesus gave us a health path to walk on. It has been said an ambulance-load of times that "the church is not a museum for saints, but a hospital for sinners." Not true. It is Jesus the Great Physician who makes sick people well. The church keeps well people from getting sick again. The church is not intended to be an infirmary for sick people, but a health club, a wellness center where people come to get well and stay strong so that they can take on the powers and principalities of the world.]

> *Life is a great bundle of little things.*
>
> Oliver Wendell Holmes

Jesus' ministry was marked by two principle characteristics, biblical scholars are now telling us. Jesus had a food ministry, and Jesus had a health and healing ministry.[10] Jesus' threefold preaching-teaching-healing methodology for ministry has as much to say and do with our bodies as with our minds and spirits.

Jesus' health teachings did not come out of nowhere. Jesus' health and healing ministry stood in the tradition of his ancestors. In Hebrew the name Raphael means "God has healed."

The archangel Raphael appears in the book of Tobit as one of the seven angels who enter and serve before the glory of God (Tobit 12:15). Since Raphael is the one who brought the young Tobias to meet Sarah, leading to the most erotic passage in the Catholic Bible (Tobit 8), Raphael is sometimes referred to as the "angel of happy meetings." Gregory called Raphael the "Remedy of God" with a mission of healing and health.[11]

The Bible teaches a God of life and health, a God who sends angels and archangels like Raphael to assure our happiness and health, our wholeness and wellness. The integration into the church of wellness ministries is long overdue.[12] Issues of health and healing, which the modern era moved progressively to the side until they became sideshows, must be moved from the "side-aisles"[13] (where they now nervously stand) to the center aisles of our faith communities.

Things have gone too far when the business world is doing more to promote wellness among its employees than the church is doing among its parishioners. Only 2 percent of USAmerica's corporations said they did not see a need for health promotion programs.[14] If a similar poll were conducted of USAmerican churches, one wonders what the results might be. Even hospitals are acknowl-

> *Jesus went throughout Galilee, teaching in their synagogues, preaching the good news of the kingdom, and healing every disease and sickness among the people.*
>
> *(Matt. 4:23 NIV)*

edging the importance of the spiritual in the healing process through the increasing number of chaplains being hired as part of the healthcare team.[15]

The promise of God is health and wellness. Faith in God is physically good for you. Denying God is bad for your health. The first undisputed mention of disease in the Bible includes the words "I am the LORD who heals you" (Exod. 15:26). There is healing for you today. [God's eye is not hazy that it cannot see. God's ear is not heavy that it cannot hear. God's hand is not hampered that it cannot save. God's heart is not hardened that it cannot heal.] The healing dimensions to the

> **The figure of the Crucified invalidates all thought which takes success for the standard.**
>
> *Dietrich Bonhoeffer*

gospel are neglected at our peril. Indeed, from a biblical perspective, health and salvation are the same phenomenon; they are different ways of talking about the same thing. The Greek word *soter* means both "savior" and "healer."[16]

Or as William Tyndale demonstrated over and over again in his pioneering 1525 translation of the Bible from Greek into English, "health" and "salvation" are synonyms: "And his father Zacherias was fylled with the holy goost / and prophisyed sayinge: Blessed be the lorde god of Israhel / for he hath visited and redemed his people. And hath reysed vppe the horne off health vnto vs / in the housse of his servaunt David. . . . And to geve knowlege off health vnto hys people / for the remission of sinnes" (Luke 1:67-77).[17]

True health and healing involve restored relationships with nature, with God, with one another, and with ourselves. That is why it is increasingly being asked of all believers: "How can you *not* pray for the sick?" That is why it is increasingly being asked of ordained ministers, "If you don't take a whole view of the person, who will?"

The modern era convinced the church to relinquish its healing and healthcare roles to M.D.s (or more precisely "M. Deities") and other scientific health providers. In fact, the "clinical model" of "pastoral care" judged ordained ministers according to how well they derived their skills and deferred their authority to the medical community. R. D. Laing has critiqued more memorably than most this "defer and refer" syndrome whereby the church defers to the therapeutic and refers the needy to sources of authority and healing systems other than the Christian faith:

> If they go to a Christian priest, the priest will probably refer them to the psychiatrist, and the psychiatrist will refer them to a mental hospital, and the mental hospital will refer them to the electric shock machine. And if that is not our contemporary mode of crucifying Christ, what is?[18]

Ordained ministers must reassert their role as practitioners of healing rituals. They must be comfortable with themselves as ritual makers[19] and with all that ritual making means with regard to health and healing.

The church is a living witness to the fact that health is not an individual accomplishment but a communal responsibility. Health (or if one comes to rest in a politically correct position, "temporarily abled") is not an individual achievement at "pushing the right but-

> **Bless the LORD, O my soul,**
>
> **and do not forget all his benefits—**
>
> **who forgives all your iniquity,**
>
> **who heals all your diseases.**
>
> *(Ps. 103:2-3)*

tons," but God's mysterious gift of love shown to all of God's creation. That is why there is no one healing procedure outlined in the Scriptures, but rather a variety of healing practices and methods—prayer (1 Chron. 21:9-27), seven-day sabbaticals (Num. 12:13-15), body-to-body resuscitation (1 Kings 17:21-22; 2 Kings 4:32-37), dips in a pool or river (2 Kings 5:14-19; John 9:7); spit-plasters (John 9:6), oil anointings (Mark 6:13), handkerchiefs (Acts 19:12), laying on of hands (Luke 13:13; Acts 9:17-18), and so forth. Faith was not even a requirement for Jesus' healing (Luke 22:51; Matt. 12:22), nor was recognition of who Jesus is (John 5:1-16; John 9). True belief or correct standard operating procedures were not requirements for Jesus' healing.

What is a healthy lifestyle and health-giving personality? We postmoderns are engaged in what Faith Popcorn calls a "hyper-quest for health."[20] Concern over polluted water, pesticide-contaminated soil, air that allows us to see what foul substances we are breathing, food that disguises the carcinogenic substances we are eating all testify to a postmodern preoccupation with healthier living and healthier habits. People are taking charge of their health ("self-health care is the future"),[21] and the Gospels provide a guide as to how this might look.

It is as important for the church to see itself as a health community as it is for the church to become a healing community. This will entail a paradigm shift from the current preoccupation with brokenness and recovery to an orientation toward health and wholeness. Too much time is spent concentrating on illness and not enough on wellness. [Before God revealed "I am the LORD who heals you," God promised that "I will put none of the diseases on you" (Exod. 15:26 NKJV). From the very beginning, God rated health above healing. It is time for the church, more known for "sickness care" than "health care," to do the same and focus its attention not on what is wrong, but on what it loves and values and appreciates.] Better futures are born not by fighting the wrongs so much as by fashioning the rights.

There is nothing people will not do, there is nothing people have not done to recover their health and save their lives. They have submitted to be half drowned in water, half cooked with gasses, to be buried up to their chins in earth, to be seared with hot irons, to be crimped with knives, like codfish, to have needles thrust into their flesh and bonfires kindled on their skin, to swallow all sorts of abominations, and to pay for all this as if to be singed and scalded were a costly privilege, as if blisters were blessings and leeches were a luxury.

Oliver Wendell Holmes

This book is an attempt to shift our focus from woundedness to wellness.

What belongs at the center of the healthcare system? Not hospital doctors (or chaplains), but healthy persons and communities. The current healthcare system is organized around the treatment of illnesses. The healthcare system of the future will focus on the creation of healthy individuals and communities and in keeping those entities healthy through preventive medicine and wellness principles. As one doctor wrote on the chart of a patient who died, "He failed to fulfill his wellness potential." Gustavus Emanuel Hiller was a German Methodist preacher who wrote at the turn of the twentieth century on "The Christian Family." In this book he argued that a Christian physician should be as involved in preventive medicine as curative. The physician should call in the home "at least once a month" even when there is no sickness, to "discover such deficiencies as may prevail in matters of hygiene; to instruct, to chide, to cheer, . . . "[22] The physician was expected to be a blessing to the family's physical, mental, and spiritual well-being.

When the seventh-century English cleric, Herebald, almost died after he fell in a horse race and fractured his skull, St. John of Beverley and an anonymous physician operated together, one through his skills at prayer and intercession, the other through his skills as a bonesetter. The Venerable Bede carefully chronicled the parameters of both procedures, and the limits of each.[23] As the story was retold by their respective communities, the religious world emphasized the miracle of the saint while the medical world stressed the manual dexterity of the physician.

The Jesus Prescription for a Healthy Life attempts to join together again what the world has put asunder.

***
Laugh a Lot
***

When Jesus laughed, the universe convulsed in songs of old joy and new hope.

Wait a minute. It never says in the Bible "Jesus laughed." It says "Jesus wept."

Jesus, like Jeremiah and other prophets before him, was moved to tears. This shortest verse in the Bible—"Jesus wept"—comes very close to deserving its own chapter as one of the ten things Jesus did to stay healthy and stay off the best-stressed list.

Before we drain melancholy out of

> *Then it seemed to me the whole Universe smiled. And joy entered both by hearing and by sight.*
>
> *Dante's* Paradiso *(27.4-6)*

every song, consider this. Why did Jesus weep? Jesus "endured the cross," the Bible says, "for the joy set before him" (Heb. 12:2 NIV). Jesus wept that we might . . . what?

Here's the second shortest verse in the Bible: "Rejoice evermore" (1 Thess. 5:16 KJV). What is the end of our discipleship, according to Jesus? Not some leaky-eyed exit, but a wide-eyed entrance into "the joy of the LORD" (Neh. 8:10) and the "exceeding joy" we find in God (Ps. 43:4).

That is why there are more Second Testament references to joy than there are to weeping, mourning, anger, sadness, and distress put together.[1] The angels announced Jesus' coming with these words: "See—I am bringing you good news of great joy" (Luke 2:10). It is likely that for many people the first sign of this "good-news-great-joy" Jesus was him laughing. One biblical scholar (Arthur Dewey of Xavier University), in exploring Jesus' oddball, off-the-wall humor, says that "There is more of David Letterman in the historical Jesus than Pat Robertson."[2]

> ### God has made me laugh, so that all who hear will laugh with me.
>
> *Sarah*
> *(Gen. 21:6 NKJV)*

I

Where is the proof that Jesus laughed? Jesus Laugh-a-Lot is everywhere in the Gospels. The layers of humor that were embedded in his teachings have been difficult for us to find for the same reason that our kids find it hard to laugh at our jokes—and Jesus is two thousand, not twenty, years distant from us. What child of a baby boomer, on hearing Jerry Rubin's 1976 quip "I'm famous. That's my job." catches the humor?[3] Scholars spend a lifetime hunting and understanding the word games, dreadful puns, and verbal sleights that

Shakespeare scattered throughout his earliest and bloodiest tragedy, Titus Andronicus (1593–94).

Jesus' humor didn't send people rolling in the grass, to be sure. He wasn't a stand-up comic, or some first-century Erma Bombeck (*When You Look Like Your Passport Photo, It's Time to Go Home* [1991]; *Family: The Ties That Bind . . . and Gag!* [1987]; *If Life Is a Bowl of Cherries, What Am I Doing in the Pits?* [1978]; *The Grass Is Always Greener Over the Septic Tank* [1976]) or a more boomer-appealing Cynthia Heimel (*If You Leave Me, Can We Come Too* [1995]; *Get Your Tongue Out of My Mouth, I'm Kissing You Good-bye* [1993]; *If You Can't Live Without Me Why Aren't You Dead Yet* [1991]; *But Enough About You* [1986]). But his hearers would have laughed occasionally, and smiled knowingly. The more scholars know about the times in which he lived, the more they appreciate Jesus' taste for world-mocking wit, outrageous aphorisms, and teasing irony.[4]

It would be too much to call Jesus a jester-magus of the first-century theological world who ruthlessly punctured the defenses of the religious establishment at precisely its most vulnerable spots. But not much too much. Jesus loved to pun and poke fun. He enjoyed poking holes in the spiritual balloons of the super-righteous, and especially those whom he knew best, the ones who often sucked the hardest on their own balloon juice. Pharisaism was a lay reform movement whose unctuous spirituality Jesus deemed too impious and humorless. Jesus espoused a lay reform movement marked by a spirituality of joy and grace that sabotaged the grave in the cause of the serious.

> **Joy is the gigantic secret of the Christian.**
>
> *G. K. Chesterton*

If we were really serious about life, Jesus taught, we would distill from life as much lip-smacking enjoyment as we could.

If we were really burdened about those in need, Jesus believed, we would have a lightness of heart with them.

If we were really serious about resisting injustice, Jesus believed, we would not be prime begetters of so many snipish injustices to one another.

If we were really serious about the present, Jesus believed, we would be a lot less glum about the future.

If we were really serious about the poor, Jesus believed, we would dance with them more and go donner-and-blitzing about them less.

If we were really serious about wrong, Jesus believed, we wouldn't live so mordantly between the wrinkles.

If we were really serious about saving the world God loves, Jesus believed, we wouldn't have such a higgledy-piggledy appearance.

For Jesus, in words that Teilhard de Chardin would use, "fullness of joy" (Ps. 16:11) was the infallible sign of the presence of God.[5] Life was far too serious to Jesus not to be laughed at and joked about. Humor was one way Jesus coddled people into truth and charged life with theological horsepower.

> *Truth-teaching is a trade he only knows by half Who does not o'er his labour sing and laugh.*
>
> *Coventry Patmore*[6]

Jesus had a ravenous appetite for puns both high ("fishers of men") and low (which in Hebrew are as much visual as oral). For Jesus, puns, jabs, and jokes are sacred teaching tools—linking us to intuitions attuned to the discontinuous bits and bites that make up soul stuff. Explanations always spoil the joke, but take Luke 13:32, where there is a "super-memorable" play on two Hebrew roots *yrš* and *šlm*. This entire passage is filled with "fantastic" puns on what in English would be the word "well"—"the artfulness" of which, scholars argue, "beggars belief."[7]

Let's explore another example, the scene in Mark where Jesus and his disciples were found in the house of Levi the tax collector, reclining at the table with many other "tax collectors and sinners." When Jesus is criticized, he playfully snaps back to all within earshot: "I have come to call not the righteous but sinners" (Mark 2:17). The word "call" *(kaleo)* is used here as a pun. Levi thought he was hosting Jesus as his guest. Jesus teases those present with the portrayal of himself not as invited guest, but as host and inviter.[8]

> **When you are hungry, sing; when you are hurt, laugh.**
>
> *Jewish proverb*

Or look at Jesus' greeting of Nathanael in John 1:45-51, which involved heavy wordplay on Israel/Jacob and guile.[9]

Jesus' famous mustard seed metaphor is both a playful burlesque and serious satire of Ezekiel's cedar imagery (Ezekiel 17; Daniel 4). You imagine that Israel resembles a mighty cedar that reaches hundreds of feet into the air? Jesus subtly chides his listeners. I think Israel is a lowly garden herb called the mustard seed that never grows above eight to ten feet tall. Using comic relief, Jesus taught the real meaning of Ezekiel's final injunction: "The LORD will bring the high tree low and make the low tree high."[10] One biblical scholar has even categorized some of Jesus' parables as "comic parables," with the prodigal son story defined as a first-century "comedy."[11]

Jesus' aphorisms (memorable one-liners) are equally humorous. Consider the new version of a well-known saying found in the *Gospel of Thomas* 3:1: "If those who lead you say to you, 'See, the Kingdom is in the sky,' then the birds of the sky will precede you. If they say to you, 'It is in the sea,' then the fish will precede you. Rather, the Kingdom is inside of you, and it is outside of you" (compare Luke 17:20-21).[12]

These are but some of the newer discoveries of Jesus' humor now being exhumed in the Gospels.[13] Much of this humor feels today like irony, but ridiculous images of camels trying to squeeze through needles' eyes or people trying to remove logs from their eyes was really more like intelligent wit. Since the

> ## In the beginning was the pun.
>
> *Samuel Beckett*[14]

devil never laughs, a sense of humor was one of Jesus' main weapons in warding off evil.

Jesus was the son of a God who, in the words of Stephen D. Moore, "creates the names of the first man and woman through wordplay ([Gen.] 2:7, 23, 3:20; compare 4:1); . . . a God who, in displaying himself to Moses, plays on his own name ([Exod.] 3:14ff)."[15] Jesus founded the church on a pun: Matthew 16:18 reads "You are *[Petros]*, and on this *[Petra]* I will build my church."[16] For a church built on a pun to be uneasy around laughter and humor (The number of pages in Doubleday's recent 7,035-page, six-volume Bible dictionary that are devoted to humor? Eleven.) is brutally ironic.[17]

II

How many stiff-backed, sober-faced, straightlaced, hard-boiled, boneheaded believers need restored to them the joy of their salvation? If there are three bones of life—the backbone, the wishbone, and the funny bone—how many funny bone implants are needed in the Body of Christ? It isn't just Baptists who are "hardshell." Where are the guardians of memory who would remind us that liturgical horseplay and the laughter of fools ("Feast of Fools," "Lord of Misrule," "Holy Fools") occupied an important part of our tradition before the Reformation?[18]

William Fry, the chief researcher in the area of the health benefits of laughing, says that people in good spirits let loose as many as one hundred to four hundred laughs a day. Do you see disciples of Jesus laughing this much—at least in public? The African-American poet and novelist Ishmael Reed, hailed as the Charlie Parker of American fiction, directed a poem in 1978 at humorless militants in the Civil Rights Movement that hits many Christian rightists right between the eyes as well:

> In your world of
> Tomorrow Humor
> Will be locked up and
> The key thrown away
> The public address system
> Will pound out headaches
> All day.[19]

Lighten up, church! "Lighthearted" need not be "light-headed," writes Presbyterian pastor David Steele in his "light-hearted" look at biblical characters called *Slow Down, Moses.*[20] My colleague Lovett Weems, quoting one of William Faulkner's novels, says the problem the church has today is that "we've taken the bells out of our steeples."[21] Faith has become no laughing matter. The smile wipes off the face when faith and Christ walk in.

We can all do things to increase our EQ (Enjoyment Quotient) easier than we can increase our IQ or even TVQ (that's television quotient or mass media appeal). The comedy writer and skewer (everyone else is the kebab) Joey Adams even made a high EQ a part of his marriage ceremony. He and his wife Cindy rewrote their marriage vows. Instead of "love, honor, and cherish," they pledged to "love, laugh, and applaud" each other.[22]

One of the best kept secrets in the history of the church is that without a high EQ, no Christian can ever achieve "sainthood." Evidence of *hilaritas* became a *sine qua non* for saints—which explains why pole-sitter Simeon Stylites has never been and will never be designated "St. Simeon." He had a slap-unhappy spirituality. His killjoy, joke-dead, sourpuss spirit killed his chances of ever becoming a saint. Umberto Eco's secret in *The Name of the Rose* was Jesus' (and Aristotle's) laughter. For Eco, the sin against the Holy Spirit is to have no sense of humor.[23]

You don't think God has a sense of humor? The French philosopher Voltaire, one of the greatest minds who ever lived, hated the First Testament (his anti-Jewishness is well known; less acknowledged is the fact that his nickname was, ironically, "Goebbels") and used it to beat on Christians. He announced one day from his home in Geneva as an accomplished fact, not as prophecy, that in one hundred years the Bible would be a forgotten book, found only in museums. One hundred years later, Voltaire's home was occupied by the Geneva Bible Society.

You don't think God

> **Euangelio (that we call gospel) is a greke word, and signyfyth good, mery, glad and ioy-full tydings, that maketh a mannes hert glad, and maketh hym synge, daunce and leepe for ioye.**
>
> *William Tyndale's 1525 prologue to the Second Testament*

has a sense of humor, even a tolerance of bad jokes, old puns, and corny lyrics?

Then why did God create me?

Or why did God make you?

Or why did God let humans make such silly-looking things as trains if not to exercise our mirth muscles? As a Kurt Vonnegut character says, God Almighty "must have been hilarious when human beings so mingled iron and water and fire as to make a railroad train."[24]

Each of us will have a different "giggliography," a different set of resources that get us laughing. Baby busters are especially notorious for their hard and hard-to-get "seriously unserious" humor. No home is complete without a laughing board on some wall or refrigerator filled with the unique "giggliography" of every member of the family.

Our "giggliographies" are shaped by our life situations as well as birth locations. The fact of laughter is not incidental, which makes a giggliography in everyone's life all the more required. If William James and Carl Lange are right, the bodily motion of laughing is, in fact, the motion of gladness and joy. In other words, we feel glad because we laugh, instead of laughing because we feel glad.[25] A "giggliography" gets us to laugh that the joy might be released.

Ever since the comedian Gallagher made airline travel into a routine, I have a whole "giggliography" associ-

> **Laughter is like changing a baby's diaper—it doesn't solve any problems permanently, but it makes things more acceptable for awhile.**
>
> *Anonymous*

ated with flying that is designed to get me to relax and to put my nerves at ease. Since I spend a lot of time flying, I spend a lot of time giggling to myself. Here are the paces my giggliography puts me through:

- As I drive to the airport, watching for the signs that indicate what exits to take, I wonder what sadist named the place where you get ready to trust your all to a creaking bunch of nuts and bolts—"Terminal."
- When I check in at the counter, I smile at the fact that this precise flight was selected for me by my travel agent because of one reason, and one reason only: it was the cheapest one available.
- When I duck my head to enter the plane, I look around at how many have booked the same flight and invariably smile because once again, I am either on a plane with 8 other passengers, or 288.
- As I slouch into my emergency exit seat, I giggle at the way the flight attendant asks those of us sitting next to exit doors to examine ourselves to see if, in an emergency, we would for any reason refuse to open the exit door. I can just see it now: The plane has crashed, fire is breaking out everywhere, and someone is sitting there saying, "I'm not opening that door. I'd rather stay in here."
- When it comes time to land, I start giggling at the airline's selection of the technical term for landing— "We are now making our final approach." On a recent shuttle a flight attendant announced reassuringly, "We'll be in the ground very shortly" (everyone hoped she meant "on the ground").
- When the flight attendant warns us not to move until the plane has come to a "complete stop," I wonder what an incomplete stop would be like.

I love Appalachian humor, the funny stories of my ancestry, and collect Appalachian jokes as part of my "giggliography." A fellow came from West Virginia to Kentucky, and he had only one shoe on. He met a Kentuckian who asked,

"Did you lose a shoe?" The West Virginian replied, "No, I found one." Or: Did you hear about the Ohioan on his way to Kentucky who got lost in West Virginia? Noticing a farmer on the hillside working the fields, the Ohioan pulled off the road, approached the farmer and asked, "How do you get to Louisville?" The West Virginia farmer replied, "Why, my wife takes me."

There are even ways to bring together Appalachian humor and airline humor. Did you hear the story of the West Virginian who contracted the flu, died, and went to heaven. St. Peter met him at the Pearly Gates, and asked how he got there. "Flu," the man replied. "On what airline?" St. Peter inquired.

Another part of my "giggliography" is cranial bits of wordplay and polyglot punning called conundrums. I collect conundrums like some people collect Barbie dolls. A conundrum means literally a riddle whose answer is a pun. Conundrums can come in story form—like the TV weather reporter who had been so wrong with his predictions that he was fired. He applied for a job in another part of the country where the interviewer asked, "Why did you leave your last job?" The weather reporter answered, "The climate didn't agree with me." Or conundrums can come in more traditional, direct forms. Here's one of my favorite conundrums: What is the difference between a bird with one wing and a bird with two? Answer: It's a matter of a pinion.

> *A joke is closer to a yoke than you think.*
>
> Guillermo Cabrera Infante,
> Cuban novelist

Deep belly laughs (or big groans) give stomach muscles about the same workout as a sit-up. Which would you rather do? One hundred sit-ups a day? Or one hundred deep laughs?

A few good belly laughs gave Norman Cousins two hours of pain-free sleep, about the same as one chemical painkiller. Which did he take?

He chose to take laughter.

III

Laughing is a physical phenomenon that gives a workout to virtually every organ in the body. Laughter is a respiratory function good for health.[26] Physiologically, it releases natural painkillers and produces beneficial chemical changes in the body. Psychologically, it lubricates the tragedies and paradoxes of life, relieves stress and may even give the immune system a boost.[27] Physically, it gives the body a "miniworkout," and its effects on the musculoskeletal system have been compared to "stationary jogging."[28] Actuarily, it often translates into a longer life, at least according to one study.[29]

Beginning with Sigmund Freud, many psychiatrists have come to view a healthy sense of humor as an excellent barometer reading of good mental health. Indeed, some researchers believe that humor is the most significant activity of the human brain because it is the one exercise that requires both sides of the brain.

Other traditions have often been quicker to see this than we have. The Jewish mime Samuel Avital contends that laughter exercises every cell in the body: "When you laugh, the whole system vibrates, a dancing diaphragm, dancing cells. All the cells are happy, and when you are happy you have a longer life. If you don't furnish your cells with this vibration of dancing, which we intellectually call 'laughing,' you are robbing them of life. So laughter is a transformer."[30] In Navajo culture, "a child is watched over constantly until the child laughs for the first time. This moment marks the child's birth as a social being. The person who made the baby laugh then provides a celebration in honor of the child."[31]

The ability to "laugh yourself back" from a serious illness is something every medical student now knows, thanks to

Norman Cousins's story of his personal bout with ankylosing spondylitis, a paralyzing, inflammatory disease.[32] The healing function of humor has not yet achieved sufficient scientific validation to fully convince the medical community. What is certain is that the "internal jogging" of laughter lightens life's desperations by releasing pain-killing catecholamines, by burning off calories, by relaxing our arteries, by secreting enzymes that aid digestion, and by stimulating the endocrine

> ***No day is complete until you hear the laughter of a child.***
>
> *Native American saying*

system. It was humor that helped Cousins to "Accept the diagnosis; defy the prognosis."

For these reasons and more, humor therapy has become a growth industry in medicine.[33] "Humor programs" are increasingly popular features of the healing sciences. A patient's medical record should include a "funny-bone history," many medical experts now argue. Some hospitals, nursing homes, and convalescent centers are now offering "humor rooms," "humor therapists," and "humor services" that include games, humor channels on TV, laughter clinics, humor books, tapes, newsletters, and so forth. There is even a twelve-page quarterly *Laughter Prescription Newsletter* that serves as a clearinghouse of humor for hospitals, hospices, doctors' waiting rooms, and other health professionals.

Businesses, some of which are beginning to offer "laughter breaks," are even using the number of times candidates smile during the interview as grounds for selecting people for potential positions.[34] Smiles get the job because smilers get the job done better than frowners.

Jesus helped other people to laugh. It might behoove us to see if we can (say, once every hour) help someone laugh.

Why is "You're really very funny" one of the highest compliments you can bestow on anyone, or receive yourself? Those who bring laughter into our lives are gifts from God. In laughter, Jesus Christ can still be found most near.

IV

If one of the ongoing challenges of eternity is to keep a straight face in the company of God, my mother is in deep trouble.

I seldom remember my mother without her "healthy" (i.e., tattered and worn) Bible. It was as if her already moley body had another black protrusion. As I saw her in every possible situation with that omnipresent Bible permanently affixed to her side, as if a very extension of her body, the only analogy I could think of was Benny Goodman. Goodman never looked complete if he was not at least holding a clarinet, and preferably blowing it. When he died in 1978, his housekeeper found him sitting upright, his clarinet fallen at his side, a Brahms sonata on the music stand in front of him. Benny Goodman died holding his clarinet.

Mother died holding her Bible. After she was admitted to the hospital, I held her hand that wasn't holding her Bible, and stroked her hair. I said, "Mother, I've got to make a decision. You remember that preacher from Atlanta you liked so much? I'm supposed to preach for him tomorrow. I don't want to leave you. Yet I don't want to disappoint him, especially since the evening event is part of his doctoral project. I'll only be gone twenty-four hours. Unless you tell me otherwise, I'll keep the appointment."

Mother flicked her hand, which meant both that she understood and that I should go. I bent over her broken body, and prayed a short prayer in her ear. Then I stroked her forehead a few more times, and left.

> ***Delight yourself in the LORD.***
>
> *(Ps. 37:4 NIV)*

I only got as far as the nurses' station. Something kept pulling me back, as if I were on a leash. I thought at the time it was because I wasn't sure Mother knew I would only be gone for twenty-four hours. As I returned to her cubicle, I arrived at the same time a nurse walked in to take Mother to her room. I introduced myself, explained my dilemma, and apologetically defended my decision. I then asked if I could call the nurses' station every couple of hours and keep track of Mother's condition that way.

"Sure you can. In fact, why don't you ask to speak to me. I'm working a double shift tomorrow, and so I'll be with your mother for a bulk of the time you're gone."

"Wow. What a godsend. What a gift. To whom should I ask to speak?"

"Just ask for Joy."

"Your name is Joy?" I asked incredulously. "Mother, did you hear that? God sent you a nurse named Joy to help you make it through the night. That's a word we both need to hear right now because neither of us is feeling a lot of joy right now.

"Mother, isn't it wonderful that God has sent you an angel named Joy to guard over you through the night. Isn't that so providential? Shouldn't we praise God for that? You remember, Mother, it was you who taught us three boys the 'Nehemiah Principle.' You taught us never to forget the 'Nehemiah Principle': 'The joy of the LORD is your . . .' "

> *Our mouth was filled with laughter, and our tongue with shouts of joy.*
>
> *(Ps. 126:2)*

I paused for a second. Mother, as if suddenly plugged into an invisible source of megawattage, lit up and finished the verse with cut-glass clarity: "strength." She smiled. I kissed her and walked out into the night.

These were the last words Mother ever spoke. On the way to her hospital room, she went into a coma from which she never emerged. She died the next day.

Mother was literally ushered into eternity on the wings of this verse: "The joy of the LORD is your strength" (Neh. 8:10). Moth-

> *He who sits in the heavens laughs.*
>
> (Ps. 2:4)

er had so marinated her life in God's Word, when all else was gone—she may not know what year it was; she may not be able to identify a pen; she may not remember the name of her eldest son—one thing remained: the joy of the Lord.

Perhaps I am mistaken above. The Bible was less an extension of her body, than she was an extension of it. She had so lived the Word of the First and Second Testaments that her life became a Third Testament.

Mother met her Lord singing a song of joy. Mother got the joy-germ fever from Jesus, who gives this condition of infectious peace and joy to every open and willing heart.

* * *

CHAPTER TWO

Hang Out with Friends

* * *

Jesus stays off the best-stressed list by nourishing in his soul a sense of belonging. He does not dam the rush and flush of feelings, but enters into relationships fully and participates wholly in life—whether in their pain or pleasure, bitterness or blessing, trials or triumphs. Jesus has eyes to see, ears to hear, and a heart to break.

Jesus invests in friendships. His capacity for intimacy is immense. He has a communal spirituality. He grows spiritually in his awareness of the divine through relationships, and draws strength from his encounters with people, especially through and with women.[1] He even calls us to be, not his servants, not his disciples, not even his blood relatives, but friends. Now "I call you friends" (John 15:15 GNB).

The word *friend* comes from an Old English word *freond,*[2] which means one who is loved or free. Jesus came to show us how much we are loved, and to set us free. God did not redeem us intellectually but relationally. God comes to us through relationships, and Jesus' sayings and doings instruct us in the sacredness of relationships. Jesus walks into our lives not as a system of doctrine or as an answer to life's questions, but as a friend and companion who sticks closer to us than any sister or brother.

Jesus is in a love relationship with God. When the apostle John says "God is love" (1 John 4:8), he is communicating the ways in which God is a relationship, even a friendship. The gospel is not about living a moral life. The gospel is not about living. the "good life." The gospel is about living life "with the living God."[3] Obedience is not in the biblical sense "doing what you are told." Obedience is living relationally, even "indivisibly" with the Holy One so that one honors, upholds, receives, and follows all that God is and all that God is calling us to become.[4]

If Ivan Illich is right in arguing that the key component in friendship is self-limitation,[5] then God's foundation for friendship with us was laid in the self-emptying of the divine in the incarnation. The quality of God's love, and the quantity of ways we enjoy touching God and experiencing the divine, is what Jesus came to reveal and fulfill: "No one has greater love than this, to lay down one's life for one's friends" (John 15:13).

Isn't this, after all, why we shun relationships—with God, with one another, with ourselves? Every relationship leaves you with a limp. But Jesus taught a faith that cannot be lived outside a web of relationships, some strands of which tear away at you while also lifting you upright. In biblical ways of thinking, you cannot discover who you are, much less become who you are, without friends.

At the same time Jesus casts a wide net for followers, he creates a fine net of relationships close to him that he calls "disciples." He gathers around him a group of friends, what became a type of Jesus Teamnet. Jesus brings together these disciples, Mark tells us, in order "that they might *be with him*" (Mark 3:14 NIV, italics mine). Does anyone really think these disciples were but professional colleagues? Jesus' contemporaries don't think so. They accuse him of jammin' with his friends, of spending too much time with his buddies.

Jesus chooses his closest friends with care. He even turns some down who wanted "in." The Gerasene demoniac, after he

> **When I'm sick and tired and hungry, Lord,**
>
> **Stand by me.**
>
> **When I'm lost and sad and lonely, Jesus,**
>
> **Stand by me.**
>
> **When I'm sinking in the battle,**
>
> **O thou who canst not lose the battle,**
>
> **Stand by me.**
>
> **When I'm old and gray and feeble,**
>
> **O thou Lily of the Valley,**
>
> **Stand by me.**[6]

is healed, asks to join the Jesus Teamnet and travel with the band of disciples. But Jesus tells him no. "Return to your home, and declare how much God has done for you" (Luke 8:39).

As the history of the Jesus Teamnet reveals, Jesus loves being cosseted by the rituals of mutual friends. These rituals feature physical demonstrations of affection, not because one needs friends (that's a modern concept), or because one needs to be touched (as true as that is), but because life is to be lived in relationship,

The fifth cup of tea between friends is the best.

Chinese proverb

and an infrastructure of rituals is vital in maintaining relationships. Jesus' ritual life with his disciples connects each
with the other and all with the beyond. Rituals of friendship
express our identity, and make sense of the story of our lives.

Some scholars argue that John 5:1-14 may be our only look
into Jesus' "hidden years" for precisely this reason. At the pool
of Bethesda, strangely enough, no disciples are with him. On
this sole basis it has been argued that this incident took place
before Jesus' public ministry. Jesus then told this story to his
disciples, who in turn recast it in a more homiletic form.

Jesus' contemporaries not only criticize him for spending
too much time with his friends, they also condemn his
choice of friends. As today, people in Jesus' day try to define
him by the company he keeps—tacky people, street people,
odd people, deformed people (Mark 2:15-17). His eating
habits are condemned as atrocious: Not only does he always
seem to be eating with "tax collectors and sinners," he also
eats with the poor, the crippled, the blind, and the lame,
even an unnamed woman who caresses his feet while he
dines at someone else's house (Luke 7:36-50). More than
once Jesus is denounced for deviant patterns of social relationships. He proves them right: At the moment of his
death, he befriends a criminal.[7]

Jesus' friendship network remains one of the least studied
aspects of his life. His friends Lazarus, Mary, and Martha, for
example, Jesus visits over and over again. In the story of
Mary and Martha, we find Jesus smack in the midst of their
everyday existence—chatting, bickering, washing dishes.
Clearly, Jesus never removes himself from ordinary life,
which he defines as "eating and drinking, buying and selling, planting and building" (Luke 17:28). He never loses the
common touch, or disconnects from routine ways of living
or unsophisticated ways of thinking.

Amazingly, Jesus leaves the safety of Bethsaida and
returns to Bethany, even after an all-points bulletin has been
issued by the Sanhedrin for his arrest if he ever sets foot back
in Judea. Why? Why does Jesus hurriedly walk thirty miles
through the Judean wilderness, up one of the steepest and

most treacherous roads in the Middle East—the infamous Jericho Road? Why does Jesus leave a successful Galilean ministry, risking arrest and execution, to return to Jerusalem? Why does he ignore the begging of his disciples not to go back into Judea, and their warning that if he does he will be killed?

Because Lazarus, his friend, is sick and has need of him (John 11:1-44).

In fact when Lazarus, who may be Jesus' best friend, dies, Jesus cries (John 11:35). Loyalty and love for a friend trigger the events that led to Jesus' death.

Jesus is careful to tell his friends how much they mean to him: "You are those who have stood by me in my trials" (Luke 22:28). Friendship was not always an easy path, either for Jesus or his disciples. Jesus' friends fought among themselves, asked insulting questions, and abandoned Jesus when he needed them the most.

But even when Jesus' friends desert him, he does not desert them. Nor does God desert him. Raymond Brown observes how Luke takes pains to point out that even in his crucifixion, God does not allow Jesus to die in isolation. Jesus is strengthened by three sources: Simon of Cyrene, the daughters of Jerusalem, and a crowd of people who beat their breasts (Luke 23:27).[8] Jesus testifies to a God who could be influenced by the concerns of friends. As parents are moved to act by the pleas of their children, Jesus teaches

> *For the mature person, the Tao begins in the relation between man and woman, and ends in the infinite vastness of the universe.*
>
> Tzu Ssu, Ancient sage

his disciples, so God too is moved to act by the pleas of God's friends.

John 20:24 is to my emotions one of the saddest verses of scripture. It reads simply, "Thomas . . . was not with [the disciples] when Jesus came." If Lazarus is Jesus' best friend, Thomas may be Jesus' pest friend. Where is Thomas that night when Jesus makes his first post-resurrection appearance?

No one knows. Maybe he is ashamed to show his face after deserting Jesus. One strong suspicion is that he is so mad at Jesus for dying he curls up in a corner and stews. Perhaps it is out of that anger that Thomas laid down some conditions that Jesus would be required to meet before he would believe in a risen Christ (John 20:25).

Whatever causes him to stop hanging out with the other disciples, the fact remains: Thomas missed it! Because he disconnects himself from his friends, Thomas is not there for one of the magic moments in the life of the disciples—Jesus' first post-resurrection appearance. The rest of the disciples are no less distraught or fearful than Thomas. They huddle together behind closed doors, the Scriptures read, "for fear": "The doors were shut where the disciples were assembled, for fear . . ." (John 20:19 NKJV). But the rest of them don't stop huddling together.

I

Why the immense popularity of TV shows like *Cheers, Seinfeld,* and *Mad About You*? Because the characters never seem to do anything but hang out. They lure us through "time porn,"[9] the tease of a life with enough time and leisure for the friendships that we all covet and know we need but don't seem to make a priority.

Why has the Internet taken off so explosively? For the same reason the *agora,* or marketplace, was a staple in ancient Greece (from at least the sixth century B.C. to the fourth century A.D.). In an AIDS-afflicted, riots-riddled, drive-by-shootings world where personal interaction between the species has become risky, networked computer environments provide a safe place where people can go and hang out.

This could also explain the popularity of greeting cards with definitions of "a friend" like: someone who will keep your secrets and never divulge them—even if tormented, or tempted with chocolate; someone who will quietly destroy the photograph that makes you look like a beached whale; someone who knows you don't know what you're talking about but will let you reach that conclusion independently; or someone who goes on the same diet with you—and off it with you, too.

Postmodern culture, with its high degree of computerization and its low protection of traditional family arrangements, makes friendships "the most secure reality," in French scholar Pierre Babin's words. "The relationships of the future will be those of friendship and small groups."[10] Forty percent of all adults are single now, a larger percentage than at any time in this century. While Jesus views marriage as the basis of social relations (Mark 10:2-12), he also addresses life outside of marriage (Luke 10:4; Mark 10:29). In fact, the story of Jesus' True Family (Matt. 12:46-50; Mark 3:19-21, 31-35; Luke 8:19-21)[11] culminates in the aphorism "whoever does the will of God is my brother, and sister, and mother" (Mark 3:35). Friendships outside of marriage loom larger in our future than forecasters ever anticipated.

The psalmist implies that the cynical and scornful sit by themselves (see Psalm 1). And those who sit by themselves, as Francis Bacon saw so vividly, "those that [lack] friends to open themselves unto, are cannibals of their own hearts."[12] As Jethro said to Moses when he was trying to do everything by himself and not asking for help from his friends, "You will wear yourself out" (Exod. 18:18 GNB).

Friends can save your life, literally. A variety of diverse tests and reports from around the world now demonstrate that warm social ties and secure relationships can boost immune functions, improve the quality of life, and lower the risk of dying from cancer, coronary artery disease, and other physical and mental health conditions at any age.[13] Studies have even shown that people can increase their life span and decrease their susceptibility to illness by participating in small groups.[14]

In fact, our need for friendships is so deep that the lack of social support networks may be a partial reason for the differential death statistics among men and women. Take a poll of midlife men you know. Ask them who their close friends are. How many have played their lives so close to the vest that they find themselves having to admit: "I don't think I have any close friends."

Men at the top of the corporate ladder may have "everything"—expansive homes, expensive cars, exclusive clubs, expense accounts. But the climb up that corporate ladder is usually a costly one to relationships. First friendships get placed on back burners. Then friendships become strategic business relationships and "power lunches." Finally, friendships become unnatural and artificial. Materially overloaded, but relationally anorexic, corporate executives have spent so little of their lives investing in friendships and rituals of solidarity they may have dramatically and haphazardly shortened their lives through the loss of an emotional capacity for friendship.

> *Without friends no one would choose to live, though he had all other goods.*
>
> *Aristotle*

When asked about his friendships, the president of a prestigious educational institution paused, stared into his glass, and muttered, "I haven't any."[15] Rich in associates and acquaintances, he was nevertheless poor in friendships. Research has shown that men do not give one another affection; men do not talk to one another about intimate things;

men do not nurture one another; men do not have complete or whole relationships.[16] There is a lack of genuine immediate friendships among men, not to speak of lifelong friendships. That is why so many men, when they reach the top, hit rock bottom.

What does it profit, Jesus said, if you gain the whole world and lose your soul?

What does it profit, if you gain the whole world and spend your life in an office?

What does it profit, if you gain the whole world and spend your days on a golf course?

What does it profit if you gain the whole world, and never know your children?

What does it profit, if you gain the whole world, and never have a best friend?

What does it profit, if you gain the whole world, and can't kiss the joy, much less "let a joy keep you" (in Carl Sandburg's words)?

What does it profit, if you gain the whole world, and never consider the lilies, much less smell the roses?

What does it profit, if you gain the whole world, and lose your soul?

In contrast to women, middle-aged male talk is noticeably lacking in connectional language and relational speech.[17] It is men's awakening to their relational incontinence and emotional incompetence that has precipitated the current resurgence of "male-bonding" workshops and the Promise-Keepers movement. Men are finding it necessary to go back to square one to be shown how to be open and vulnerable in relationships in order that they might develop the capacity to form close attachments.

One Atlanta business entrepreneur has even made a successful living out of this male disability. For a price of about twelve hundred dollars, he promises to find "buddies" for successful executives who have more money to buy friends than time to build friendships. "It's tough to admit," sighs one patron of this service, "but men have a very difficult time establishing relationships with other men, other than for business reasons. . . . It's not like the days at the fraternity."[18]

Social isolation affects the immune system. People who have extensive networks of friendships are better able to fight off disease and trauma than those who don't. "The single most important psychological factor . . . from our data and across a decade of research studies in hundreds of people across the country is that the more and stronger the personal relationships, the better the immune function," argues Ohio State University College of Medicine psychologist Janice Kiecolt-Glaser, who along with her immunologist-husband Ronald Glaser have shown how stress can suppress the immune system to the point of risking physical illness.[19]

The first experimental study of any animal's immune response to long-term stress and social trauma revealed that monkeys whose "affiliative behavior" was friendly and open in the midst of psychological and social stress suffered less immune decay than those who were less friendly and tactile.[20] Breast cancer patients who had few friends, who were separated/divorced, or who described themselves as "lonely," demonstrated reduced levels of immune activity.[21]

A pioneering article by Stanford University Medical Center's David Spiegel demonstrates that treatments for cancer that feature social support mechanisms produce the greatest survival rates and health returns.[22] Another study reveals that the greatest success rates for weight-loss programs and exercise regimens are those that enlist friends and family as partners.[23] In short, friendships and social bonding actually served as a kind of inoculation against immune deficiency and decay while undergoing difficult circumstances.

One reason some people sojourn at mental health centers, and others don't, is because when some reach a point of crisis in their lives, they are alone. The Amish, whose sense of community is so strong that they ask one question of any proposed innovation—"What will this do to our community?"—are only one-fifth as vulnerable to depression as other USAmericans.

A connected life is not only a contented life, it is also a healthy life. A network of healthy relationships is one of the best vaccines for depression, disease, and even death. God's plan for healing often comes by what has been called "The Titus Touch." "But God, who comforts the depressed, comforted us by the coming of Titus" (2 Cor. 7:6 [NIV]).[24]

Who is this Titus who helps heal Paul of his depression? Titus is a gentile Christian of Greek origin who becomes Paul's chosen traveling companion and trusted coworker. When trouble arose in the church in Corinth, Paul sends his Titus, who demonstrates his pastoral skills by resolving the difficulties. Healing for Paul does not come until "the coming of Titus." Because Paul lets someone "Titus Touch" him, even when that someone is an "underling," an apprentice, he experiences the healing power of friendship.

You and I need Tituses. You and I need to be Tituses. "People come into your life for a reason, a season, or a lifetime," Michelle Ventor observes. "When you figure out which it is, you know exactly what to do."[25] Will you let someone "Titus Touch" you? Will you receive the "Titus Touch"—even from such unlikely Tituslike sources as a child, or employee, or enemy?

In Wilmington, North Carolina, an administrator of United Theological Seminary watched in horror as a young man reached under the seat of his car, pulled a gun out of a paper bag, and shot and killed himself after a routine fender bender. Moments before, he had spoken these words to the administrator. "I have no one."

II

Jesus just didn't "hang out" with friends. He "hung out," period. Look at how many "chance" meetings take place in Jesus' life—for example, his high-noon encounter with the woman at the well near Sychar (John 4:6-26). One of the Papyrus Gospels gives this interesting scene of Jesus and the disciples loitering in the temple: "And he took them (the disciples) with him into the place of purification itself and walked about in the Temple court. And a Pharisaic chief priest, Levi (?) by name, fell in with them and said to the

Savior: Who gave thee leave to tread this place of purification and to look upon these holy utensils without having bathed thyself and even without thy disciples having washed their feet? . . . I am clean. For I have bathed myself in the pool of David." Jesus answers that the officious priest, because he is so preoccupied with being properly set apart, has unknowingly bathed himself in the same impure water in which "dogs and swine lie night and day" and in which "prostitutes also and flute-girls anoint, bathe, chafe and rouge." Jesus and his friends, by contrast, "have been immersed in the living water."[26] Over and over again, Jesus is loitering, loafing about and then something happens.

The poets among us have called this "holy loitering." In fact, Charles Baudelaire believes that only the loiterer (*flaneur*) could truly experience modern life. Whatever you call it, every one of us needs to do it. Jesus seemed to sense that we do not live in a cause and effect universe. We live in a "connectional" universe where it is not just electronic communication that makes any place every place—as in the television ad for MCI where a child star chants "There will be a road. It will not connect two points. It will connect all points. It will not go from here to there. There will be no there. We will all only be here."

In connectional systems the here and the there are the same. In connectional systems, nothing ever just happens. There is no such thing as "happenstance." Everything is connected to everything else. Literally, in life, nothing ever just *happens*.

Part of the meaning of Jesus' parable of the friend at midnight (Luke 11:5-8 "yet because of his persistence he will get up and give him whatever he needs") had a marvelous manifestation in the life of Ludwig van Beethoven. One night Beethoven was aroused from sleep by someone loudly banging on his neighbor's door. The person hit the door hard four times, then paused, then hit it another four times, then paused, then again, and again. Finally he or she quit.

But Beethoven couldn't quit. Those four raps kept beating in his head over and over again until he could not get back to sleep. The only way he finally got them out of his head was to write the Fifth Symphony, where those same four beats occur over and over again, always in new and fresh guises.

Physicists are dismantling virtually every boundary that separates our innermost being from the universe itself. You can no more own any part of your body than you can own a breath of air. We are a part of the universe, and the universe is a part of us.

The paradox of living in a connectional universe is this: On the one hand, the more we know, the more vast the universe appears, the greater God seems, and the more insignificant we appear in it.

We live in a universe that is so mysterious, astrophysicists shake their heads in bewilderment. Speaking of the inability of science to measure the "blackness" of matter in space, University of Washington astrophysicist Bruce H. Margon admits "It's a fairly embarrassing situation to admit that we can't find 90 percent of the universe."[27]

We live in a galaxy so big that a light ray takes 100,000 years to go from one side to another—traveling at 186,000 miles per second. And how many galaxies did God create?

We live in a universe that contains at least two hundred billion billion stars—put in terms of grains of sand, that's all the sand on all our beaches.

We live on a planet where one teaspoon of water contains about three times as many atoms as the Atlantic Ocean contains teaspoons of salt.

Physicist Charles Misner believes that this "is why Einstein had so little use for organized religion, although he strikes me as a basically very religious man. He must have looked at what the preachers said about God and felt that they were blaspheming. He had seen much more majesty than they had ever imagined."[28]

On the other hand, the more we probe the mysteries of the universe, the more we comprehend what is going on around and within us, the more awesome and transcendent God gets, yet the more immanent God becomes and the more the divine seems to surround us. The more insignificant the individual appears in the vastness of the universe, the more we realize how great an impact even insignificant things can have, including and especially the human species, through such things as chaos theory's sensitive dependence on initial conditions.

"There, *but* for the grace of God go I" is heard as a compassionate comment by most people. Actually, it is an adage that fulfills T. S. Eliot's vision of hell—a place where "nothing connects"—and as such ought to be banned from every lip. In a connectional universe, the only response to people dangling from one of life's hooks is not "There but for the grace of God go I" but "That's me!" "There I am." It takes only one dysfunctional parent or incident of child abuse. Our response to degradation and misery must be not "There, *but* for the grace of God go I" but "There, *by* the grace of God, go I," "There go I, *for* God's grace," and "There am I, *with* God's grace."

Everything is connected to everything else. Even the emergence of AIDS, some are arguing, is not disconnected from the destruction of the tropical biosphere. "Unknown viruses are coming out of the equatorial wilderness of the earth and discovering the human race. It seems to be happening as a result of the destruction of the tropical habitats. You might call AIDS the revenge of the rain forest."[29] Agatha Seuyimba, diocesan health official for the Ugandan Namirembe Anglican diocese working in HIV education and prevention in this continent so ravaged by AIDS: "We may not all be infected, but we are all affected. We say, take care of your neighbor."[30]

III

Some of us complain about living in "waiting rooms." Jesus spent his ministry waiting in living rooms.[31] Those moments when nothing seemed to be happening, those were the moments for him most pregnant with possibility.

Jesus hung around with Martha and Mary while they cooked and cleaned; he arrived early for dinner parties and stayed late; he strolled when he might have ridden or sailed to his destinations. How ironic, Charles Handy has written, that "Some people have work and money and too little leisure time, while others have all the leisure time but no work and no money. Those who are idle do not see it as a privilege but as a curse because they tend to be at the bottom of the heap."[32] Generation X has a "slacker" reputation because many of its members have chosen to have time instead of money, or, in the words of *The Official Slacker Handbook,* "If you refuse to be a cog in our economic machine you become . . . a detached spectator with a lot of time on your hands."[34]

> ***It does no good to think moralistically about how much time we waste. Wasted time is usually good soul time.***
>
> *Thomas Moore*[33]

But one great social phenomena of our day is the way in which people from all ages and socioeconomic groups are dropping out of the "rat race" and "downshifting" their lives, opting for lower-stress, lower-cost, laid-back lifestyles and embarking on all sorts of spiritual quests.[35] Like Jesus, who exited a successful career as a skilled craftsman for a soul journey, there are more and more USAmericans who are taking lower paying jobs, reducing work hours, quitting work outside the home, and quitting work entirely for a simpler life that invests more in family and friendships than in money and work, as well as valuing life that promotes social purpose and civil empowerment.[36] Even Juliet B. Schor, who researched *The Overworked American,* is now studying this shift in the American psyche where hung-up workaholics are turning into hanging-out, higher-life pilgrims.[37]

The role of open-ended, unstructured time and places where kids can just "hang out" is being seen as more and more critical in the development of a healthy imagination.[38] In a world where "leisure" time is no longer "leisurely," but filled to the brim with activities and agenda, stimulation has replaced imagination. Without "hangouts" and "waiting rooms," whether in our communities or on our calendars (Advent, Lent), there can be no living room for the imagination. Without "hanging out" with God, there can be no outpouring of God's spirit. Without the ministry of presence in people's lives, there can be no presence of ministry.

Electronic culture has turned even "waiting rooms" into work rooms. The "office of tomorrow" bears some striking resemblance to the sweatshop of yesteryear, and the "technological whip" held over white-collar workers surpasses any control or monitoring mechanisms conceived in the past. Curt Supplee, in a January 1990 *Washington Post* article, says "We have seen the future, and it hurts." The Informational Age can enslave people in their work and homes more than even the Industrial Age. The next time you are in an airport, watch travelers with pagers, modems, cellular phones, fax machines, and PCs dangling from every part of their bodies. Electronic collars can enslave us even more powerfully than iron chains or hot brands.

> *Life's an affair of instants spun to years.*
>
> John Masefield

Poet Ted Hughes writes about a thrush on the lawn, whose delicate legs are "triggered to stirrings beyond sense" and who can suddenly, with the stab of its beak, "overtake the instant and drag out some writhing thing."[39] Jesus is a master at "overtaking the instant." The most cramped and crabbed spaces he opens onto the most roomy and revealing vistas into this world and the next. Jesus can sink a well just about anywhere and get a gush of spiritual truth. Jesus starts anywhere, with anything, and then moves from there to ultimate, universal truth.

After his resurrection, Jesus was strolling along the road to Emmaus when he met two disciple friends. Even though they did not recognize him, Jesus hung out with them long enough to talk spirituality, eat dinner, and change their future. But it was not until much later, when the disciple friends finally figured out who their strollmate on that road really was, that the transformation took place.

Every moment matters. And every moment has a long fuse. Even a lifetime fuse. Sometimes an eternal fuse.

* * *
Play Out the Child in You
* * *

An old *New Yorker* cartoon shows a sidewalk Santa Claus standing next to his artificial chimney, ringing his little bell. Facing him is a little girl who says, "I don't believe in Santa Claus anymore." To which Santa replies, "That's okay. I don't believe in *kids* anymore."

Who has not seen that cartoon in living color? Once every year the Christian religion gathers its family members around a crib. One Christmas Eve, the Sweet clan went to the early "family service." The littlest of the lot (three years old) was so entranced by the decorations, the pageantry, the candle-lighting ceremony, the birthday cake for Jesus, the lighting of the Christmas tree, that when the service ended he couldn't contain himself. He went up to every adult he could find, tugged at whatever was hanging down, and said "Merry Christmas." "Merry Christmas." "Merry Christmas."

I watched in amazement as the adults responded, "Why, thank you young man." "Thank you, son." "Thank you. Aren't you a nice boy?" But not one person wished the child a Merry Christmas in return. Not one. No one at that church on that Christmas Eve outwardly deemed a child worthy of a "Merry Christmas."

The irony is deep. Researchers of congregational life have not been able to find a more key point of entry for new members than children's ministry. "Let the little children come unto me," we recite obediently, but then add this codicil: "But not on Sunday morning at eleven A.M., and only thereafter at appointed times." Our adult-centered churches hear "childlike" for "children" in Jesus' unconditional announcement that the kingdom of God belongs to *children.*

> **Anyone who forsakes the child he was is already too old for poetry.**
>
> *Stanley Kuntz,*[1] *Poet*

I shall never forget a congregational prayer that was offered one Sunday morning in church. When the pastor asked for prayer requests, one third-grader spoke up and asked for prayers for his little brother. "He's got strep throat." The congregation giggled.

Why? Wasn't that child's prayer as honest and holy as anyone else's. Who else could ask for prayer and get chuckles instead?

Children bring out the best in a culture, and the worst. Ask those mothers who were so self-absorbed that they permitted the death of their children. Children are bringing out the worst in postmodern culture, which is proving itself profoundly hostile to children. Princeton sociologist Robert Wuthnow tells of this exchange between a middle-class mother and her child:

"Mommy," Julie Baiens remembers her nine-year-old son calling to her one evening as she sat bent over her word processor in the corner of the family room, "if you had a dog, and you really loved this dog, and you worked real hard to earn the money to buy him the fanciest dog house and the best dog food, don't you think it would be better if once in a while you played with that dog?"[2]

The case can be argued that we even live in a world where children suffer the most. *Utne Reader* chose as "The Top Censored Story of 1993" the ways in which being a child is hazardous to your health. The accompanying article states that according to a 1993 report from the United Nations Children's Fund, nine out of ten young murder victims in the industrialized world are Americans. In the preface to his book *Sex, Economy, Freedom, and Community*, Wendell Berry offers sixteen simple principles as the keys to understanding our educational system today. The last three numbers pertain directly to how we treat our children:

> XIV. The main thing is, don't let education get in the way of being nice to children. Children are our Future. Spend plenty of money on them but don't stay home with them and get in their way. Don't give them work to do; they are smart and can think up things to do on their own. Don't teach them any of that awful, stultifying, repressive, old-fashioned morality. Provide plenty of TV, microwave dinners, day care, computers, computer games, cars. For all this, they will love and respect us and be glad to grow up and pay our debts.
>
> XV. A good school is a big school.
>
> XVI. Disarm the children before you let them in.[3]

The annual *Kids Count* report, funded by the Annie E. Casey Foundation, tracks gruesome trends among the nation's 63.8 million children, chronicling the devastating economic and social disparities among 6 percent of them (four million, 84 percent, of these are Black or Hispanic) who are growing up in neighborhoods where poverty, violence, unemployment, and dropping out of school are a way of life. The poverty rate among children in the U.S. is twice that of any other industrialized nation. And a Tufts University study revealed that twelve million American kids go to bed hungry each night.[4] A 1994 study by the Families and Work Institute finds that 35 percent of in-home or "family" day care is so deficient it poses a mental and physical health hazard to children's development. It is true that 60 percent of the eighty thousand childcare centers are housed in churches. But only 15 percent are actually run by the religious institution that houses them.[5]

Just before every airplane's passengers board, an attendant invites all "Children Traveling Alone" to board first. In a world of "Children Traveling Alone," the church needs to be a haven of refuge and its leadership should be children's escorts through life.

Andrew Sandstrom gave the eulogy for his father, a chaplain at a Minnesota Lutheran nursing home. The son told how as a child, while greeting people after worship and waiting to go home, he would twist himself into his father's billowing black robe and bury his head in the soft folds of his vestments. "I thought that being inside that robe," Andrew confessed through the tears, "was the safest place in the world."[6]

It is the church's job to make it so.

I

When Paul instructs the Corinthians to put away childish things (1 Cor. 13:11), some of them took him too literally. They, and others in the early church, virtually deprive Jesus of a childhood. One moment he is a soundless baby in the arms of Mary, threatened by Herod with the worst child abuse imaginable. The next moment he's a young man come-of-age debating deep theological issues with the rabbis in Jerusalem. The early church was even less concerned about Jesus' childhood than about his birth. Little happens between Jesus' birth and baptism, from Bethlehem to the Jordan River, that interested the Gospel writers.

However, the little that we are told about Jesus' infancy suggests that the child was father to the man. Matthew tells us that Joseph gave him the name "Jesus" (1:25). In Pales-

Because, Lord,

you no longer have arms to welcome the
children of the earth,

especially people seen as outsiders,

like those who were pushed aside by the
apostles

when they crossed your path long ago.

You no longer have knees for them to sit on,

and eyes to look at them,

words to speak to them

and to make them laugh,

or lips

to kiss them tenderly.

But the wonder is

that you need us,

you need me,

imperfect mirror that I am,

to reflect a few rays of your love.

Michel Quoist[7]

tinian Jewish culture, paternity was *legal*, not biological. By giving Jesus a name, Joseph made himself Jesus' father in the eyes of the law, squelching possible rumors of the child's illegitimacy. He took the boy as his son, though he knew he was not his own, and though he had nothing more to go on than a *dream* that the child was "from the Holy Spirit" (Matt. 1:20). Matthew says that Joseph was a "righteous" man (1:19).

How much of Jesus' confidence and self-respect is traceable to Joseph's "righteous" act? Because Joseph was a good and decent man, Jesus felt chosen and beloved. Perhaps Joseph gave Jesus more than a name. According to Mark 6:3,

> *I am content and at peace.*
> *As a child lies quietly in its mother's arms, so my heart is quiet within me.*
> *Israel, trust in the LORD now and forever!*
>
> *(Ps. 131:2-3 GNB)*

Jesus himself was an artisan before he became a rabbi. Joseph taught Jesus a trade. Perhaps it was from Joseph that Jesus learned the most important lesson of all—a lesson about God.

Scholars have noticed that Jesus is peculiar among his contemporaries in referring to God as "Father" (*Abba*). Feminist theology has taught us how difficult it is for people to form a positive image of God as "Father" if their own fathers have been absent, neglectful, or abusive. That Jesus imaged God as Father tells us much about his relationship to Joseph. When Jesus hung on the cross, and prayed "Father, forgive them!"—was he remembering the good man who had taken as his son a child that he knew was not his own?

Jesus, the man, was also the child whom Mary nurtured and loved. Though Mary was poor and of low estate, she carefully "wrapped him in bands of cloth, and laid him in a manger" (Luke 2:7). The practice of swaddling newborn infants was widely regarded in the ancient Near East as a sign of *maternal nurture*. Solomon boasts that his mother wrapped him in strips of cloth at his birth, for in no other way should a king come into the world (Wisd. of Sol. 7:4-5). The angels said that this would be the sign that a savior had been born—"a child wrapped in bands of cloth and lying in a manger" (Luke 2:12). Incongruous sign! The child of a poor girl wrapped up like a king and lying in an animal's feeding trough. During every Christmas, why do Christians not find themselves looking for the sign—a poor child treated like royalty by his or her mother.

In spite of the censoring of Jesus' childhood or "hidden years," as biblical scholars like to call them, Jesus demonstrates in his adult life that he never censored the child in him. Jesus demonstrates the ability to view the world from the eyes of a child. Jesus shows a high regard for children, and even though he develops no theology of childhood, he does lift up the carefree and childlike trustfulness that does not worry about the morrow (Matt. 6:25-34) as representative of faith itself.

As some would put it today, Jesus let the child within come out.[8] He never became "a-dull-tified." He always conquered the CPT (Can't Play Today) syndrome. Some extrabiblical accounts (for example, the *Infancy Gospel of Thomas*) say that as a child Jesus made clay pigeons and told them to "fly away." Years later, Jesus was still making mud pies—this time putting mudpacks on the blind and sick and telling them to go away and be healed.

Jesus made friends with the children of the families of his neighborhoods. He loved to play with children, and, plopping a child in their midst, insisted his disciples take time to play with children. He told a parable of a children's game and chanted a children's rhyme (Matt. 11:16-19; Luke 7:31-35). He prized children's spiritual experiences, and touted a child's ability to trust and love.

One biblical scholar has even argued that the mysterious "beloved disciple" is actually a child named John from Judea (probably Jerusalem) whom Jesus met by the Jordan River with John the Baptist, perhaps the same child who brought Jesus the five loaves and two fishes. In this rather fanciful scenario, what first began as a teacher/disciple relationship between Jesus and John soon grew into something more intimate until "Jesus adopted the youngster as his own son in a strong affectionate relationship."[9]

The pride of place and affection Jesus gave this child when they were together caused jealousy as well as embarrassment among the disciples. They felt they deserved to be at Jesus' side, not some young person. Yet "Jesus insisted that the close presence of such a 'child' was a public example of spiritual childhood and of the reversal of the typical human patterns of domination and authority."[10] Whatever the background behind "the beloved disciple," Jesus' celebration of childhood left his contemporaries perplexed and even angry:

> *I am not young enough to know everything.*
>
> Sir James Barrie,
> *Author of* Peter Pan

> They all were looking for a King
> To slay their foes, and lift them high
> Thou cam'st a little baby thing
> That made a woman cry.[11]

No wonder children respond to Jesus with such warmth and trust. Children loved him and flocked to him. Don't we sing about the children ("Into the city I'd follow the children's band, waving a branch of the palm tree high in my hand."), who greet Jesus and put him first in their hearts on that first Palm Sunday ("All glory, laud, and honor, to thee, Redeemer, King, to whom the lips of children made sweet hosannas ring")? Isn't it the boys and the girls who first come out of their homes and cut down branches to cheer and carpet the parade path of Jesus of Nazareth? When Jesus says "Become as little children," he is really saying "Let me come into your life and minister to the frightened, lonely child within you." Children know better than anyone that Jesus can heal the bruises and scrapes and lacerations of life, binding up our wounds just as surely as did the Samaritan in Jesus' parable. Children know better than anyone to ask Jesus and to hope for impossible things.

The biblical emphasis on the "inner child" should not enourage sentiment that pulls us away from those aspects of Jesus' personality that actually put away childish ways. We are right to linger over things in life (for example, those lovey-dovey scenes in movies) over which children want to fast forward. Indeed there are things about Jesus that chill our spines—his lashing out at the moneychangers (Matt. 21:12-13); his face set like flint in steadfast determination (Luke 9:51); his protection of children to the point where Jesus' language became harshest when dealing with those who would subvert the faith in the young or feeble—"it would be better for you if a great millstone were fastened around your neck and you were drowned in the depth of the sea" (Matt. 18:6).

There was no arrested development in Jesus' ministry. The eighteenth-century German mystic Novalis

> ## The man old in days will not hesitate to ask a small child seven days old about the place of life, and he will live.
>
> *A "new saying" of Jesus according to* Papyrus Oxyrhynchus *654 4:1* [12]

wrote in one of his notebooks: "A child is a good deal cleverer and wiser than an adult—but the child must be an ironic child." Jesus' admonition that his disciples become as wise as serpents but as innocent as doves was his version of "ironic children."[13]

→You must never grow out of childhood, Jesus taught. You grow into childhood. South African theologian Michael McCoy argues that the heart of Jesus' teachings is a dual movement toward and from the child. At the same time the Christian seeks to grow outward into the fullness of Christ, McCoy argues, the Christian seeks to return inward to a state of childlikeness. If one only goes outward without going inward, one lapses into "arrogant adult autonomy." If one only goes inward without going outward, one enters a state of "infantile helplessness" and "irresponsibility."

This dual movement sets up a creative tension: At the very point when Christian people feel grown up, autonomous, and secure in their adulthood, they most need to rediscover the child within (Mark 10:15). And when they feel most dependent, vulnerable, and weak, then they most need to know that they can grow into "the measure of the stature of the fullness of Christ"[14] (Eph. 4:13).

Take a childlike approach to life, Jesus argues. Treat everyone you encounter as a love child. Children are much closer to the spiritual world—the world of angels, omens, demons, signs, and voices—than adults. Have you yet become like

> *In the beginner's mind there are many possibilities, but in the expert's there are few. . . . The real secret of the arts: always be a beginner.*
>
> *Shunryu Suzuki* [15]

children, Jesus asks over and over again? Jesus insists his disciples undergo a process of "de-adultization." He seems to have an instinctive distrust and distaste of all species afflicted with adulthood, which Andre Malraux's *La Condition Humaine* (1934) describes in classic fashion:

> "You know the phrase: 'It takes nine months to make a man, and a single day to kill him.' We both know this as well as one can know it. . . . May, listen: it does not take nine months, it takes fifty years to make a man, fifty years of sacrifice, of will, of . . . of so many things! And when this man is complete, when there is nothing left in him of childhood, nor of adolescence, when he is really a man—he is good for nothing but to die."[16]

The Irish poet George William Russell, who wrote under the pen name of "A.E." makes an astute and tantalizing observation: "In the lost boyhood of Judas/Christ was betrayed."[17]

II

We don't know much about what kind of childhood Jesus had. We don't know much about what kind of father Jesus had. For all the "Madonna" depictions there are of Jesus and Mary, there are only a handful of paintings of Jesus being held by Joseph. Did Joseph midwife Jesus' birth? Was Joseph kind and loving, or was he distant and unaffectionate?

The Bible doesn't answer such questions directly, although in Joseph's initial resolve to quietly divorce his pregnant betrothed, he was both the proper Jewish boy and a compassionate person. When Joseph dies, probably by the time Jesus is in his early twenties, Jesus has to assume responsibility for supporting the entire family of four younger brothers and a number of younger sisters. This may have been why Jesus' mother and brothers come from Nazareth to another town where Jesus is preaching, presumably to put an end to the disrepute and disdain this head of the family is bringing upon the family and the name of Nazareth.

"A little child shall lead them," Jesus said. Many Native American tribes (for example, the Pueblo people) looked to wisdom from the eldest and youngest in their midst, since both were seen as closest to the mind of God. "When was the last time a church had children consult with its Administrative Board?" asks Philip D. Schroeder, a specialist in children's ministries.[18] Our reluctance to make outsiders such as children "insiders" is well-founded: They are sources of disruption as well as innovation, their models and muses different from ours.

The nonproductive activity known as "play," the kind of play that makes a culture, the kind of play that makes a church, is the natural habitat of children. To participate in "child's play" is to enter the joyful process of learning about the world while experiencing it. The play of prose in motion, which we call poetry, is what helps us retrieve "the lost child within" according to Irish poet Brendan Kennelly.[19]

Theologian Horace Bushnell was one of the first moderns to argue that the true worship of God was more found in play than in work. "Religion must, in its very nature and life, be a form of play—a worship offered, a devotion paid, not for some ulterior end, but as being its own end and joy."[20] In spite of the inspirational message borne by the gate at Auschwitz—"*Arbeit Macht Frei*/Work will make you free"—it is play that sets us free and spawns creativity. Rather than "Work at it" admonitions, postmodern culture is beginning to understand that marriages or manufacturing or

> **Truly I tell you, there are no grown-ups in heaven.**
>
> *Jesus* [21]

ministry go better when based on a play paradigm ("Play at it") rather than a work paradigm ("Work at it").

Scientists David Bohm and F. David Peat in their book *Science, Order, Creativity* insist that "Thought is generally considered to be a sober and weighty business. But . . . creative play is an essential element in forming new hypotheses and ideas."[22] Roger von Oech, in his wonderful book on creativity *A Whack on the Side of the Head*, has concluded that play is the very essence of creative thought. Von Oech studied thousands of people and the sources of their most creative moments. He found there were two dominant settings. First, intensive, focused thought about a problem. Second, play or "toying around" with a problem.

Necessity may be the mother of invention, but play is certainly the *father*. . . . Most of life presents you with a win/lose proposition: If you don't win, you lose. This is true for most games and sporting events, elections, coin tosses, bets, arguments, and the like. When you play, however, a different logic is at work: a win/no win logic. This is an important difference because

> *No soul on this road is such a giant that it does not often need to become a child at the breast again.*
>
> *. . . For there is no state of prayer, however sublime, in which it is not necessary often to go back to the beginning.*
>
> Teresa of Avila, Sixteenth-century Carmelite nun[23]

it means that instead of being penalized for our mistakes, we learn from them. Thus when we win, we win, when we don't, we learn. This is a nice arrangement; the only thing play costs is the time to do it.[24]

❧ Play may also be the very essence of healing. "Play as Healing" is but one chapter in Dorothy G. Singer and Jerome L. Singer's pathbreaking *The House of Make-Believe: Play and the Developing Imagination.*[25] More than a book, *The House of Make-Believe* is a summary of forty years of research. It is also a book that highlights the tremendous shift from modern to postmodern. In the modern era playfulness was frowned on as "adolescent" at best, "childish" at worst; opportunities to exercise one's imagination and playfulness were carefully circumscribed.

In contrast, play has come to be seen as more an investment than a waste. Postmodern culture is much more playful than its predecessor, to the point where the Singers document the healing properties of pretend play: Imaginative play helps children deal with their confusion and the incongruity of the world about them; play helps children integrate new developments into their lives—death, birth, divorce, and so on—and develops in them an imaginative consciousness. Adult modes of play—punning, riddles, or games—bring creativity and originality to life.

For this reason it is almost as important that people play together as that they pray together. This is one reason "the ologies of play" keep resurrecting themselves every decade, challenging the church to become a playing community and discover new playmates and playgrounds again. The kingdom of God that Jesus talked about was a kingdom of play, where life and laughter come naturally without expensive equipment, clothes, or skills.

In God's kingdom of play, joy constantly comes into play, and indeed stands as the chief measure of existence. One Maryland pastor talks about his periodic need to get in touch with "the beach side of me" (Thomas Short) where play is an end in itself and not a means to something else. Theologian

Rubem Azevedo Alves has suggested that Jesus' admonition *"unless you become like children"* was really another way of saying that *"life is to be played and play is to be lived."*[26] All work and no play is what made Judas so unstable.

In presenting a kingdom of play, Jesus made play with a whole host of inherited notions—about the Sabbath, about strangers, about who's first and who's last. Jesus loved to play with words and metaphors (for example, his less-is-more parables are simply an extended metaphorical playground of word pictures: "the kingdom of heaven is like . . . "). Parables were more than a form of teaching for Jesus. They were a ritual form of play (in many ways, ritual is space for communal play). In Jesus' amazing parables, which were part paradox, there were portrayed upside-down, topsy-turvy truths which, because everything is inverted, posed then and continue to pose today tremendous threats to every status quo.

> *The understanding of atomic physics is child's play compared with the understanding of child's play.*
>
> *David Kresh*

I had just spoken to a group at Camp Sumatanga outside of Birmingham, Alabama, where I mentioned that Ben & Jerry's Ice Cream consistently ranks as one of the one hundred best places to work in America. One reason for this designation is that Ben & Jerry's employs an executive with the official title "minister of joy." This person's job description is to plan parties for the employees, and to generally see that there is a spirit of play and joy that pervades the work environment. Opening the door to my room after the lecture, I found under the door a signed "Certificate of the Right to Play." It has become one of the prized possessions of my life.

The full text of the certificate can be found on pages 66-67.

In his marvelous book *Landscapes of the Sacred,* Belden C. Lane defines sacred place as "storied place." "Tell me the Stories of Jesus" is a favorite children's song. Stories are to the child's soul what air is to human lungs. Thanks to the

> **God invented man because he loves stories.**
>
> *Hasidic saying*

new interest in storytelling—storytellers include authors, poets, rappers, singers, novelists, playwrights, actors, physicists, musicians, ministers, teachers, secretaries, psychologists, professors, and others—children can breathe more freely. Jesus loved to tell stories, and he loved to listen to stories. Our story and Jesus' story are not two separate stories, but part of the same story: To be a Christian means to decide to live inside the Jesus story, not outside it.

I would not go so far as composer Richard Meale, who argues that it is stories, not individuals, that are important. But it is the stories that continue. In his opera *Voss,* there comes a point where it is said that stories end, but life goes on. But Byron counters, "No. It's stories that go on forever."[27]

But I would go so far as to agree with the suggestion that the ultimate judgment will be for "the divine Tale Teller to fall asleep while we remember and tell the story of our lives."

> **Children are innocent and love justice; while most of us are wicked and naturally prefer mercy.**
>
> *G. K. Chesterton*

By this certificate know ye that

Leonard I. Sweet

is a lifetime member in good standing in

THE SOCIETY OF CHILDLIKE PERSONS

and is hereby and forever entitled to

☆ **WALK** in the rain, **JUMP** in mud puddles, **COLLECT** rainbows, **SMELL** flowers, **BLOW** bubbles, **STOP** along the way, **BUILD** sandcastles, **WATCH** the moon & stars come out, **SAY** hello to everyone.

☆ **GO** barefoot, **GO** in adventures, **SING** in the shower, **HAVE** a merry heart, **READ** children's books, **GET** silly, **TAKE** bubble baths, **GET** new sneakers, **HOLD** hands & **HUG** & **KISS** & **DANCE**.

☆ **FLY** kites, **LAUGH** & **CRY** for the health of it, **WANDER** around, **FEEL** scared & sad and mad and happy, **GIVE** up worrying and guilt and shame, **STAY** innocent, **SAY** yes & no and the "magic words," **ASK** lots of questions, **RIDE** bicycles, **DRAW** & **PAINT**, **SEE** things differently, **FALL** down and **GET** up again, **TALK** with animals, **LOOK** at the sky, **TRUST** the universe, **STAY** up late, **CLIMB** trees, **TAKE** naps, **DO** nothing, **DAYDREAM**.

☆ **PLAY** with toys, **PLAY** under the covers, **HAVE** pillow fights, **LEARN** new stuff, **GET** excited about everything, **BE** a clown, **ENJOY** having a body, **LISTEN** to music, **FIND** out how things work, **MAKE** up new rules, **TELL** stories, **SAVE** the world, **MAKE** friends with the other kids on the block, and **DO** anything else that brings more happiness, **CELEBRATE, RELAX, COM- MUNICATE, LOVE, CREATE.**

☆ **ENJOY** health, joy, pleasure, abundance of grace and self-esteem!

☆ **ENJOY** courage, balance, spontaneity, passion, beauty, peace, and life-energy.

☆ Furthermore, the above named member is hereby officially authorized to frequent beaches, meadows, mountaintops, swimming pools, forests, playgrounds, picnic areas, summer camps, birthday parties, circuses, cookie shops, ice cream parlors, theaters, aquariums, zoos, museums, planetariums, toy stores, festivals, and other places where children of all ages come to play, and is always encouraged to remember the motto of The Society of Childlike Persons:

IT'S NEVER TOO LATE
TO HAVE
A HAPPY CHILDHOOD!!

Hell will not be a pit of eternal fire, but the terrible realization that God is bored. We have not only wasted our lives but God's time as well.

Heaven, on the other hand, will be seeing a smile on God's face and a twinkle in the divine eye, to know that the Holy One is delighted with our story. "Well told," God will say.[28]

Well told, good and faithful storyteller.

In one of Nikos Kazantzakis' short stories, an old man is dying. He trembles with guilt and shame for his lapsed life, and upon his death he continues the trembling as he goes before the Judgment Seat of God. He sees a large bowl of aromatic oil in front of Jesus, who, without a word, dips a sponge into the basin and begins washing this contrite man clean of his guilt and shame.

Then Jesus speaks these words: "Don't bother me with that stuff anymore. Go over and play."[29]

Go and play.

* * *
Walk a Daily Dose of LSD (Long, Slow Distances)
* * *

Jesus was a walker. He relied on the power of his own legs to get him places. Walking by the Sea of Galilee, he calls two pairs of brothers to leave their living and walk with him (Luke 5:1-11). "Come, follow me" was the summons of a walker. As his footsore disciples could attest, Jesus' closest friends were those who "walked" the hard, harrowing but happy path of life with him.

Indeed, Jesus used "walking" as a metaphor for the life of faith, as we have continued to do to this day (Crop Walk, Emmaus Walk, Walk for Alzheimers, MS Walk, Greenpeace's Greenwalk, L.A.'s CityWalk, Good Friday Walks for Justice and Peace, to name but a few). Some of the most powerful words that resound through the centuries, whether in the Scriptures in the figure of the lame beggar at the Beautiful Gate of the Temple (Acts 3:1-10) or on television in the figure of Amahl (from *Amahl and the Night*

Visitors) are these: "I can walk." The *Gospel of Peter* shows Jesus walking out of the tomb on Easter morning, assisted by two angelic figures. Here is the resurrection imagined as physical therapy: learning to walk again. The joyful walking in the way of the Lord is the essence of a healthy lifestyle.

One can never know for sure the road Christ will travel. . . . Those who follow in his footsteps soon find themselves going in directions they may not wish to go.[1] Jesus contrasted the wide gate and the narrow gate—the wide gate was the main, broad gate that provided everyone entrance to the city. The narrow gate was the small passageway that allowed only pedestrians and small animals to pass through. If you would enter heaven, Jesus taught, you must walk through the narrow gate.

Perhaps Jesus inherited his love of walking from his mother. Even though Mary was not required to go to Bethlehem for the enrollment, she must have volunteered to accompany Joseph on what was for her "great-with-child" condition an arduous and unnecessary ninety-mile trip to Bethlehem for the census. In fact, Israeli archaeologists have unearthed an octagonal church structure outside Jerusalem they believe was erected by early Christians to hold the rock on which a pregnant Mary rested on her way to Bethlehem.

Or perhaps Jesus' love of walking was set after he was born, when Joseph and Mary took their newborn to Egypt as refugees to avoid Herod's plot on his life. After all, the first two or three years of Jesus' life were spent in transit from Nazareth to Bethlehem to Jerusalem to Egypt and back to Nazareth.

However he learned it, Jesus was a great walker. He didn't retire to the desert, like John the Baptist before him. Nor did

> *If you don't take care of your body, where else are you going to live?*
>
> Mabel Boggs Sweet

he headquarter some place and wait for people to come to him, like some other teachers of his day. He went to where the people were, and made for towns, villages, and cities in multicultural Galilee, in Palestine, and in pagan country.

Jesus didn't get around by riding donkeys and camels or sitting in carriages and chariots. He wandered "throughout all Judea" (Acts 10:37 NKJV). He walked-talked "in the Jewish countryside and in Jerusalem" (Acts 10:39 REB). He was an expert practitioner of what the medical community calls "LSD"—long, slow distances. He hiked the distance from Jerusalem to Capernaum, which would be like you or me walking from Milwaukee to Chicago. Luke was apparently so impressed with this aspect of Jesus' life that he structures the last half of his Gospel as one great journey to Jerusalem.

Jesus walked everywhere. He even walked on water.

Jesus exercised. He didn't have a Nautilus or Soloflex to keep in shape. But he did have his legs. Jesus and his father Joseph were builders, artisans who worked with stone and wood to construct things, perhaps working side-by-side to rebuild the city of Sapphoris. Jesus' hands were not soft and smooth, like virtually every painting portrays them. Jesus' hands must have been weather-beaten and calloused—from nearly thirty years' general contracting work and from three years of helping his friends to fish—rowing rugged boats by night and pulling in and mending heavy nets by day.

When Jesus gave up construction work for teaching, healing, and preaching, he kept in good physical shape by walking. Jesus knew the meaning of exercise. What other athletic or physical activities he may have engaged in, we do not know. The world of sports and the Greek games, one of the two hallmarks of the Greek way of life (philosophy being the other), doesn't manifest itself in the life of Jesus, and there are no allusions to athletics in the parables of Jesus.[2] While there is nothing negative to sports per se in the biblical witness, the silence of Jesus on "sports" while he affirms "sport" (for example, fishing), "physical education" (walking), and play (dancing, singing, games)[3] may suggest a caution about the unhealthy hold sports can have on the imagination, an abuse that Chrysostom later voiced in near-contemporary terms:

> If you ask Christians who is Amos or Obadiah, how many apostles there were or prophets, they stand mute; but if you ask them about the horses or drivers they answer with more solemnity than rhetors.[4]

Without any evidence of involvement in competitive sports, we do know that Jesus used the number one exercise regimen to keep in shape, the almost "shockingly effective strategy" of lifelong fitness and a healthy lifestyle: walking.[5]

I

It is now a medical commonplace that inactivity is in and of itself an independent risk factor for disease, just like smoking or drinking. Do you smoke? If so, then you can expect to lose ten to fifteen years of life.[6] Do you drink? There are physical consequences that come from this decision. Do you exercise? If not, then you also can expect to lose years of life. Physical activity acts as a powerful protective against disease. And the most recommended form of physical activity is walking. Walking delivers only half or a quarter of the jolt to aging joints and muscles as running or other high-impact aerobic exercise. Walking can be done with children in strollers, or walking can be done on a lunch break in work clothes.

"Fitness walking" is defined as walking twenty minutes per mile for three miles at least three (at best five) days a week. Thirty minutes of walking, fifteen minutes per mile, three times a week, gets your heart rate in your target zone, which is the minimum you need. That's not a lot to ask in order to enjoy a decreased risk of 40 to 50 percent for heart-related illness than that of sedentary individuals.[7] One study, reported in the *New England Journal of Medicine,* evaluated fifteen hundred middle-aged men for heart disease, and found that the risk of heart attack was 66 percent lower among men with the highest level of physical activity (defined as more than 2.2 hours per week of walking, running, bicycling, swimming, participating in ball games, and similar activities) compared with sedentary men. Similarly, those who scored highest on cardiorespiratory fitness scales had 65 percent lower risk of heart attack.[8]

Walking enlists the involvement of the entire body. It is the exact opposite strategy of "spot reducing," which does not work, argues Covert Bailey, because if it did, "people who chew gum would have skinny faces."[9] Precisely *because* walking is so efficient to the whole body, it gets the blood moving, muscle groups flexing, the immune system pumping, and oxygen circulating faster than most other forms of exercise. In fact, walkers traveling faster than five miles an hour actually burn twice as many calories as runners going the same speed.[10]

Most of the symptoms we associate with aging are not signs of aging, but signs of either disease or inactivity. When there is lifelong exercise of the largest organ in our body—the brain—intelligence quotients increase, not decrease, with age. The memory loss that older people talk endlessly about simply fails to show up on objective tests.[11] Weakness, frailness, and mental slowness are not unavoidable by-products of aging, but of inactivity.

> *A schizophrenic going for a walk is healthier than a neurotic on a couch.*
>
> Gilles Deleuze and Felix Guattari

Furthermore, it is never too late to reclaim strength and energy. Studies reported in *The New England Journal of Medicine* looked at nursing home residents, whose mean age was eighty-seven (ranging from seventy-two to ninety-eight).

After ten weeks of strength-training exercise, members had more than doubled their muscle strength. Walking ability increased 11.8 percent, and stair-climbing ability improved 28.4 percent. Those who didn't perform weight training had muscle strength decline 4 percent in that same period.

Whatever your age, thirty minutes of exercise a day will keep the weight down, the spirits up, the mind alert,[12] the calendar turning, and maybe even your children laughing. As the little girl said to her minister, "Pastor, if you think the Lord moves in mysterious ways, you should see my mother doing aerobics." Walking is as good an aerobic workout as jogging or sprinting, racquetball or tennis. Aerobic exercises like walking or wogging (walking interspersed with jogging) raise self-esteem at the same time they reduce stress and, by inducing sweat, help the pounds melt off like snowballs in summer. The only negative to aerobic exercise has been identified by columnist Dave Barry, who traces the word *aerobics* to two Greek words, *aero* meaning "ability to," and *bics* meaning "withstand tremendous boredom."

Since water is more the ideal environment for exercise than land, especially for those with disabilities or arthritis (a disease that affects one in seven Americans), or

> *When you walk, be aware of those who walk alongside you, behind you, before you, of those on whose efforts you now stand.*
>
> *We are surrounded, says the writer of Hebrews, by a cloud of witnesses.*
>
> Joan Puls[13]

for those who live in areas where urban air pollution makes outdoor exercise hazardous to one's health, perhaps new paradigm churches would do well to consider putting in swimming pools where people of every age, shape, and fitness level can gather for aquatic exercise, stress reduction, friendship, and fun. Whereas a significant percentage of the population cannot walk for exercise, 98 percent of the population can engage in water workouts and become "aquasizers." Water walking is at least as important an exercise program as land running.

While virtually every study shows that physical activity is one of the best ways to stay healthy and prevent heart disease, diabetes, and hypertension, not even half of all USAmericans exercise. Childhood obesity is at a thirty-year high. Of all the athletic shoes that sold in the 1980s, 90 percent never saw one exercise session. Their biggest use? Going shopping in style at the mall.

Christians are among the worst exercisers, and clergy are the worst of the worst. Ken Cooper, the founder of the aerobics movements and the head of the Cooper Aerobics Center in Dallas, says that of any professional group he sees, pastors are in the worst shape. Have you seen the "Saturday Night Live" parody of the endangered species "Middle-Aged Man" and his lounge-lizard companion "Drinking Buddy"? We must change our "couching" ways—at home and at church. "Pew Potatoes" are becoming as much a laughing-stock as "Couch Potatoes."

II

Something is wrong with a society in which a pedestrian runs more risk of injury than persons in any motorized transportation, including motorcycling. Something is wrong with a society in which almost one-third of urban motor vehicle-related deaths are pedestrians. Something is wrong with a society in which pedestrians run down on city streets account for more than twice the fatalities of all two-vehicle collisions.[14] Something is wrong with a society in which outdoor exercise may be a significant health risk because of ultraviolet radiation, ozone pollution, and generally foul air.

Recreation ministries will be a boom program for the postmodern church. Asbury Church in Charles Town, West Virginia, has purchased a warehouse and turned it into a gym as part of the church's emerging "recreation ministry" to the community. Another church decided in the interests of "good stewardship" and "mission" to abandon plans to build a sanctuary and instead built a "sportatorium," a gymnasium used seven days a week (for aerobics, after school games, basketball, and lectures), which doubles as a worship center.

New paradigm communities of faith should encourage their members to go fishing or sailing or skiing or participate in whatever athletics that provide physical and mental recreation. Robert Redford's movie adaptation of Norman Maclean's *A River Runs Through It* details the multiple linkages between the art of fly-fishing and the art of faith. Lyle Schaller, for one, has emphasized the importance of sports, exercise, and athletics ministries, already well in place in the Southeast and West, "to overcoming anonymity to creating additional entry points for tomorrow's new members to strengthening family ties to assimilating new members to increasing adult male participation."[15] Those churches who have claimed the whole person for ministry will list their ministers of recreation (or in the case of youth, ministers of athletics) alongside ministers of music, ministers of seniors, ministers of education, ministers of pastoral care, ministers of family life, ministers of videography, and ministers of food.

The least the postmodern church can do

> **When I see an adult on a bicycle, I do not fear for the future of the human race.**
>
> *H. G. Wells*

is encourage people to walk to worship, or come on bicycles. In 1951 novelist John Bayley met his future wife, novelist Iris Murdoch, when looking out a college window. He saw "a very ordinary looking girl, I thought, on an old-fashioned bicycle. I'm not sure if it wasn't the bicycle I liked most."[16] Novelist Henry Miller nominated his bicycle, the "bachelor machine," as his favorite friend.[17] How many people come to church on bikes? How many bike-friendly churches are there?

In many countries the bicycle is the most widely used vehicle for private transport. China, for example, has 250 bicycles for every car. While auto sales have flattened worldwide, the number of new bikes produced in 1992 exceeded that of new cars worldwide by almost three-to-one. Between 1970 and 1990, annual car production grew by fourteen million, while bike production increased by sixty million.[18] Similarly, worldwide sales of bicycles in 1993 outstripped automobile sales by a factor of three-to-one: One hundred eight million bicycles were produced in 1993. A sign of the future is the fourteen "Critical Mass Rides" in North America, a protest march where hundreds of cyclists ride in unison through a city's streets with the same message: "Get Off Your Assphalt."

Half of all USAmerican commutes to work are under five miles, a figure that suggests what the average commute to worship might be. Bicycling to work is becoming more popular in USAmerica with every passing year, especially in college towns with baby buster populations. The number of bicycling commuters has tripled in the last ten years, with half a million Americans riding their bikes to work the last week of March 1990.[19] Already between three and four million USAmericans commute to work on bicycles—that's one in sixty workers. According to a 1992 poll done by *Bicycling Magazine,* that figure would increase to one in five if better facilities were available.[20]

Examples of improved facilities can be found in Seattle, Washington, where buses sport bike racks, or in Portland, Oregon, where one hundred lemon-yellow bicycles are scattered around town for anyone to ride, free of charge, and drop off wherever he or she goes ("Free community bike. Please return to a major street for others to reuse. Use at your own risk." reads the license plate).[21] Palo Alto, California, is a cyclist's heaven where a forty-mile inner-city system of well-lit bike paths, bridges, and parking areas have made bike travel a favorite form of transportation and recreation. Palo Alto residents are reimbursed for business-related bike travel mileage.

Some states are even making bike paths and biking facilities eligible for transportation funds in their effort to promote bicycling as a transportation alternative. In fact, local communities are now mandated to integrate bicycling into their transit plans by provision of the 1990 Clean Air Act and the 1991 Intermodal Surface Transportation Efficiency Act (ISTEA). There is $155 billion in funding to back up this push toward nonmotorized commuting.[22]

Three signs of the future? First, an increasing number of home buyers are looking less at tennis courts, golf courses, and outdoor pools, and are wanting access to bike paths, hiking trails, and fitness centers.[23] Second, a growing number of police officers are patrolling on bicycles. "Mounties" no longer means just cops on horseback. In increasing numbers of cities it means cops on mountain bikes—in fact, there are already over three hundred "mountie" bike patrols nationwide.[24] Third, while running, tennis, basketball, and aerobic shoe sales have skyrocketed since 1980, the greatest increase in footwear sales has been in walking shoes.

III

"Walking" is not simply an outdoor exercise, however. It is a strategy for ministry itself. In fact, Jesuit scholar Kevin Wildes argues that the essence of Pope John Paul II's theology is a philosophy of truth ("phenomenology") that has as its key metaphor "walking around." Instead of lining up behind some authority or revelation, one circles life and "moves around it," experiencing life from a multiplicity of angles, until one does live out of the truth of what it means to be human.[25]

The Christian should walk about inside as well as out. Walking is an "inside" strategy as well as an outdoor one. Consider this sign at a Ford Motor Company plant: "When you don't know what to do, walk fast and look worried." Inside "walking," interior "circumambulating" (C. G. Jung's phrase for the self's "circling around" of life), and in-house "walks" (also known as Tom Peters's M.B.W.A. or "Management by Wandering Around" where the leader's central job is to wander among the employees and encourage them to do their best)[26] are means for organizations to remain healthy and vibrant.

The Christian faith is a walking gospel. If the church is to embody the "walking gospel" of Jesus the Christ, it must teach its people at least four different kinds of walking peripatetic (the method of teaching or learning while moving around): Walk-the-Talk Walking, Goalwalking, Prayer-Walking, Know-Your-Place Walking. In many ways each one of these "walking gospels" is a form of prayer, which should take place in different postures—kneeling, walking, prostrate, holding a map—and in different places—in front of schools, churches, on city streets, in church buildings, and so on.

First, Walk-the-Talk Walking. "Walking" in Latino and African-American circles today stands as a metaphor for what kind of witness one gives in one's everyday life. At a time when Christians are making such little sense of the great issues of the day as our millennium slips away, the question "Do you walk the talk?" goes right for the moral jugular. For Latinos and African-Americans, a "walking gospel" is one that eschews the air and armchair for the streets, and incarnates the Christian faith in the world, connecting the gospel to public issues. Actions can be the most powerful prayers we offer to God.

To walk-the-talk with Jesus means we walk, literally. To walk-the-talk with Jesus means we step in and walk behind Jesus. Jesus took the gospel to where the people were. Where are the multitudes today? They are inside their electronic cottages plugged in to a variety of media outlets.

The following letter was sent to Max Williams, pastor of the Scioto Ridge United Methodist Church in Hilliard, Ohio. It is dated 20 March 1995, and is quoted verbatim.

Dear Max:

Last night I had an interesting experience that I would like to share with you. I sometimes venture out among strangers to see how Jesus is working in the world. I was at a place with lots of rooms—people gathering for all kinds of purposes. One sign said "Christian Fellowship" so that's where I went.

The room was nearly packed and a lot of conversation was going on. I was drawn to a group where one young woman was really struggling. She was raised by, and lives with, a family of Satanists (unbelievable!) but somehow, Christ must have touched her because she was trying to find a way into the light. Since I was a latecomer, I don't know all of her background—but a few people were talking to her and trying to help her. I joined in and was surprised to find myself witnessing in this way—I'm usually too private about my faith (you know, don't wear that button out into the world)!

Because the room was so crowded one of the people asked if she would like to go to an Upper Room. Well I am only slightly familiar with that as a Biblical reference and I had no idea what it meant in this place (it was my first time here). Anyway, she was willing to have more privacy, so this girl and 4 others (including me) were led to an Upper Room.

I had no idea what I would do there—I am not great at quoting scripture but I do an OK job of sharing my experience with Christ, so I figured God could do His work and I'd be willing. One of the people was sort of a leader—I'm guessing he has some experience with this because he seemed to know when to move this girl forward. The rest of us gave our "amens" and shared whatever we were inspired to add.

The love and presence of Jesus in that room was awesome. We held hands, cried, prayed, gave thanks . . . eventually we were led in prayer by which this girl and one other turned their lives over to God.

I was so grateful to have been there. I always tell people that God doesn't waste burning bushes on me because I DO believe. I think, in fact, He often sends miracles—I just don't always see. I don't know what, if anything, I am to take from this experience. I feel strengthened and want to know Jesus and serve more than I have. Whether or not He has something specific in mind, well I'll keep watching, praying, and listening for His guidance.

There are more details to this story, but they aren't important to share at the moment. What I do want to share though is why I am writing this to you. I just wanted to let you know that JESUS IS ALIVE IN CYBER-SPACE. Thought that you could appreciate that! (Yes, what I am saying is that this all took place by way of computer.)

If you are interested and the Spirit moves you, I am open to further discussion. Do you suppose that one day the church might support mission work out there in C-S? There are certainly a lot of lost, searching souls there!

In Jesus' name,
Betsy[27]

The gospel must go inside to get people out-of-doors. It must meet people where they are, even on their sofas staring into a screen. This is perhaps the greatest failure of Christian evangelism and theological education today: the failure to claim the electronic media, which has become the primary teacher of postmoderns. While writing still carries the prestige of intellectual primacy, cultural primacy is fast moving toward electronic modes of communication. Tellingly, most literary novels sell only five thousand copies in hardback.

In its theology of communication, the church wears its heart on a sleeve cut in sixteenth-century Geneva. Fixated on print and fearful of electronics, the church has joined the academic elite in the most obvious, and obnoxious strategy toward an electronic culture: ritual condemnations of scuzzy taste buds and cheap shots about shallow, debilitated cravings. All our long-winded drudges haven't prevented postmodern children from falling in love with the screen as moderns fell in love with the book. Nor have we kept the postmodern academic elite from a similar love affair with the screen. Studies show there is only a 1 percent difference between the viewing habits of the best and least educated. And this gap is closing.

The church is mired in the digital dark ages. Christians stand at the bottom of the information food chain. We have yet to achieve even card-index understanding of the publishing phenomenon of the 1990s, *Wired* magazine. We have yet to hear the cries of our "unliterate" computer whiz kids: "Adults need to read to get a job to buy computers for their kids."[28] One can be as addicted to the screen (they are called "telebetics") as one can be addicted to books, and when the bloodstream circulates only glucovision, something is awry. In his discussion of the role of the screen in the evangelization of postmodern culture, novelist Walker Percy acknowledges the dangers of a culture of telebetics, but he still contends: "It would be difficult surely to imagine a more perfect instrument through which the Church can teach, inform, indeed evangelize."[29]

Second, Goatwalking. Jesus didn't just "walk around the block," biblical scholar Bernard Brandon Scott has observed. "He walked *away* from the block."[30] Jesus did more than hike. Jesus wandered. Jesus "goat-walked."

Naturalist and eco-theologian Jim Corbett, who gave this foraging for food and "free and easy wandering" through life the name "goatwalking," insists it is "biblical—even liturgically biblical."[31] After all, the Hebrews spent forty years "goatwalking" in the desert. The first people on the scene in Bethlehem, to worship and praise the newborn king, were professional goatwalkers (the goatherds and shepherds), the first to hear the news of Jesus' birth. Goatwalking involves a passage through life that is more concerned with fitting together with outdoor rhythms and inner promptings than fitting into social hierarchies and ready-made roles and expectations. A "hallowing way of life" that lives lightly on the land and ventures beyond "where the sidewalk ends," to goatwalk through life means to live by communion, not consumption; by faith, not by sight; by spiritual discernment and prophesyings, not long-range or strategic planning.

Jesus spent a lot of time simply "goatwalking" around the shore of Galilee. A roundabout, over-and-under wandering so natural to children, goatwalking is a mode of locomotion that doesn't so much cover the countryside as caress it. Goatwalkers can feel the lay of the land in such a way that the earth itself sets the course for the journey.[32] Corbett touts "goatwalking" as a form of "errantry"—of sallying beyond social establishments and expectations and living "according to one's inner leading." In the goatwalking sense errant need not be aberrant; to be "errant" is to follow a different drummer, not to be bound or rushed by social conventions. A life built on spiritual discovery, unhurried solitude, and reflective community will strike this world as much too leisurely and lax. But some things, like bread-making, are best not rushed.

There is nothing in this universe that is not in motion. Everything that exists—whether rocks on a mountainside or rockets in space—is moving. The question is not whether the motion is aimless wandering or purposeful walking. The question is whether the motion is open or closed.

Third, PrayerWalking. PrayerWalking is a spiritual exercise defined by Steve Hawthorn and Graham Kendrick as "praying on-site with insight."[33] Few people PrayerWalked more than Jesus of Nazareth. Wherever he went he kept the prayer wheel turning, and in his prayer life drew from large portions of the Scriptures he had memorized as a boy, most likely while studying under the Pharisees, a movement (strong in the village synagogues) that was likely instrumental in his knowledge of God.

Jesus not only prayed to God three times a day, as did all pious Jews, Jesus prayed over the meals he shared with his friends (Matt. 14:19; 15:36; 26:26-27). Jesus PrayerWalked by himself (Mark 1:35; Luke 5:16). Jesus PrayerWalked with his disciples (Luke 11:1). Jesus PrayerWalked the whole night long (Luke 6:12). Jesus PrayerWalked before important decisions and crucial events (Luke 3:21; 9:18, 28-29; Mark 14:35).

I engage in PrayerWalking before every speaking engagement. Early in the morning, I walk up and down the streets of my new town, claiming this street, that building, this home, that school for Christ. All the time I am praying for God's help in conveying seekers to the destination of truth. I first started PrayerWalking as a stress-reducing, anxiety-lessening technique. I had read all the medical literature that acknowledges the importance of meditation and prayer on patients, as brain waves demonstrably change when we pray.

> *Prayer is not the overcoming of God's reluctance; it is laying hold of God's highest willingness.*
>
> *Richard Trench*[34]

But in my PrayerWalking what I found was that prayer does not so much change things as prayer *is* a thing. Prayer is a material force that affects my life and my world in ways that I do not pretend to comprehend. In the words of Thomas Chalmers, "Prayer does not enable us to do a greater work for God. Prayer is a greater work for God."[35] The point of "The Lord's Prayer" is not to say it. It is to become it. And when one's entire being becomes a prayer, and one is attuned to a higher power, one may indeed raise one's health condition and healing potential to higher powers. But one also may raise one's sense of sin and anxiety level to higher registers as well. Cistercian monk Thomas Keating is right in observing that "Centering Prayer will reduce anxiety perhaps for the first three months. But once the unconscious starts to unload, it will give you more anxiety than you ever had in your life."[36]

Archbishop of Canterbury Ramsey was asked once, "How long do you pray every day?" He replied, "For one minute." "One minute? *That's* not very long." "No," replied the archbishop. "But it takes me an hour to prepare for that minute."[37] For one's life to become literally "The Lord's Prayer" for even one minute may mean that one has spent twenty-three hours and fifty-nine minutes in PrayerWalking preparation, PrayerWalking while you walked the dog, PrayerWalking while you worked in the garden, PrayerWalking while you drove your car, PrayerWalking while you studied for that exam.

Fourth, Know-Your-Place Walking. Jesus' sense of place enabled him to contextualize his ministry and reach into the soul and vitals of everyone with whom he came in contact. Wherever he was, and with whomever he was, Jesus knew their ups, he knew their downs, he knew their lower depths, and he knew their streetwise pleasures. If you are looking for a muddy-boots spirituality, it would be hard to find one that has gone on more transcultural walks or tramped more mission fields than Christianity.

Here is one simple test for how well you know your place. Can you describe how to get to your exact residence on planet Earth to an alien from outer space? Until you can, you don't know your place well enough.

Here's another exercise in Know Your Place Walking. Read the signs of your place. Run your practiced eye over your yard. When the hepaticas have huge bites out of their little leaves, what does it mean? (The deer have paid you a visit?) When there are perfectly round divots in the ground and the crocuses have been scattered all around like garbage, what does it mean? (The chipmunks have been digging up one of their life's rarest delicacies: crocus bulbs?) When the skunk cabbage has been torn up by its roots, what does it mean? (The bears have come calling?)

Jesus was a pedestrian. And pedestrians walk—sometimes here, sometimes there, sometimes hereabout.

* * *
Mind Your Thoughts
* * *

Jesus minded his thoughts. Jesus knew the power of the mind. What you are inside, he insisted, is what you become outside. One scholar argues that the original Aramaic version of Luke 11:41 reads "But first cleanse the things that are within, and behold everything is clean for you."[1] Jesus healed a paralyzed man not just by saying, "Get up and walk" but by promising "Your sins are forgiven" (Mark 2:5). A healed mind generates a healed body and a healed life.[2]

The character of our thoughts Jesus linked directly to the quality of our world.

Jesus presented new ways of thinking about what it means to be "healthy" of mind as well as body. Vegetarians maintain we are what we eat. Jesus taught we are what we think and feel. Matter doesn't matter. It is what the mind does with matter that matters. In F. F. Centore's scale of six logically distinct mind-body positions, Jesus was a second-order psychosomaticist.[3]

Jesus' sense of the interconnectedness of the body, mind, and spirit was perhaps matched in the ancient world only by Hippocrates. In his famous medical prescriptions, Hippocrates featured exercise, massage, diet alterations, and, believe it or not, prayer.

There is now proving to be such an interplay between thought, emotions, hormones, T-cells, and the immune system that scientists are questioning assumptions about "individual life" and are now arriving at the axioms where Jesus and Hippocrates started— the inseparable oneness and organic connectedness of life.

> *You are wherever your thoughts are. Make sure your thoughts are where you want them to be.*
>
> Rebbe Nachman
> of Breslov
> (1772–1810) [4]

The foundation for twenty-first-century medicine, one observer summarized, "is now education, diet, exercise and meditation." [5]

We must be careful not to enter the Third Millennium with twentieth-century science and technology but with nineteenth-century notions of mind-body relationships. [6] There is underway a biological revolution in medicine and healthcare that is redefining "sickness" and "health" [7] in terms that are almost biblical. In fact, in the new edition of the standard reference guide for mental health professions called the *American Psychiatric Association Diagnostic and Statistical Manual of Mental Disorders,* there is a new category "Religious or Spiritual Problem" that evidences the psychiatric movement's new willingness to treat religion seriously and not merely as a neurosis or delusion. [8]

The modern era separated thinking and acting. "There's nothing wrong with you; it's all in your mind" was a favorite mantra. The biomedical revolution of the postmodern era has taught us that there is such interdependence of body and mind that if it's in your mind, it's everywhere, and something is very seriously wrong with you.

Mind and body are one entity. The radical dissociation between what is thought and said and done, what the senses know and what the heart feels, each of which went its own way in the modern era, is over. The three-pound human brain, five hundred million times more complicated than our most advanced computer, is being called "the new frontier." In fact, the emergence of mindbody medicine has so exploded since the mid-1970s that *Consumer Reports* felt obliged to get into the publishing act—*Mind, Body Medicine* explores the quality of resources that deal with the impact of thoughts, beliefs, and emotions on physical health.[9]

What these resources reveal is that the associations between thought and action are less capricious than ever imagined since the Enlightenment. The motions and emotions of the soul cause the brain to release chemical messengers throughout the body. The desires of the heart trigger and set in motion the mechanisms of the mind. Thinking is the first step of acting.[10] The world as we know it—from malls to Microsoft to Mothers' Day—is the creation of thought. Truth is a function of action, which is a function of thought, which is a function of soul.

In brief, soul is the seed of thought. Your beliefs become your powers. "Cognitions" (beliefs, desires, dreams) give rise to emotional and physiological states, not the other way around. Thought has the power to create or destroy. Every thought carries with it a corresponding physiological change—and

> **The care of tuberculosis depends more on what the patient has in his head than what he has in his chest.**
>
> *Sir William Osler,*
> *The father of modern medicine*

with some ten thousand thoughts passing through the human brain each day (70,000/week, 3.65 million/year), that's a lot of biological change.

The question of how one knows when to trust the promptings of the mind and heart is now a medical issue. To acknowledge the tremendous potential of thought for good or ill is not to suppress imagination, but to watch our thoughts and imaginings even more closely. Dreams, day-dreams, and fantasies, which we are taught to check and contrast with "reality" (and never take too seriously), actually teach volumes about ourselves and our soulscapes. Rather than disregard our fears or suppress those thoughts that pop up from our unconscious, we should watch them and mind them and to some degree control them through our choice of words and images.

Studies of the best way to deal with pain demonstrate that suppressing thoughts of pain fixates the person on the pain. Paradoxically, monitoring one's thoughts of pain enables one to gain control over the pain and escape distress.[11]

Rather than deny negative thoughts or make them go away through tranquilizers, antidepressants, and addictive behaviors, the better strategy is to mind these thoughts and to pass through the pain: to see pain as a teaching place to go into rather than as a tormenting place to get away from. Stress doesn't cause illness; it's our responses to stress that make us vulnerable to illness.[12]

The costs and consequences of our thoughts and dreams are so high,

> ## As above,
> ## so below.
>
> *Jewish proverb*
>
> ## Our outer world is a reflection of inner attitudes.
>
> *E. F. Schumacher,*
> *Catholic economist*

sometimes we need to seek the help of therapists and spiritual advisors in aligning properly these spiritual sources of energy. In fact, it may be time for us to return to how ancient peoples conceived of words and thoughts—as concrete and powerful entities, magical, almost material forces that one hurled from one's being.[13]

Jesus taught this creative principle of the moral law: AS WITHIN, SO WITHOUT. We live out of the "fullness of the heart." What are we full of? Out of that fullness do we live.

Thoughts and feelings reverberate in our bodies. You don't think so? Know anybody who blushes? Blushing is not a high-octane emotion like jealousy, fear, anger, or love. Blushing is little more than an awareness that—"Oops. I know that you know that I know that you know." But that low-grade thought is powerful enough in many people to literally change the color of their skin, alter their metabolic rate, raise their blood pressure, and turn their inside organs even redder than their outside sense organ.

Or try another experiment. Blindfold volunteers in a walk through the woods. Then apologize to them that you led them astray, and their forearms brushed up against a poison ivy or poison oak leaf. Then watch as their minds are able to cause the symptoms of the allergic reaction right there on their skin, as an ugly red rash forms where the nonexistent poison plant was thought to have come into contact with their skin.[14]

> **Man is the only animal that blushes, or needs to.**
>
> *Mark Twain*

Alterations in our mental and emotional states produce alterations in our bodies. John Locke's most famous essay ("Concerning Human Understanding," 1690) needs to be reread in light of subsequent mindbody research by the likes of Stanford neurophysiologist Karl Pribam, who claims we "feel forward" in our lives—our thoughts and images precede and affect our actions.[15] Similarly, John Wesley's abridgement of Jonathan Edwards's *Religious Affections* includes Wesley's own Lockean intuition "Yea, it is questionable, whether an embodied soul ever so much as thinks one thought, or has any exercise at all, but there is some corresponding motion in some part of the body."[16]

Images act directly on the body.[17] Italian psychiatrist Roberto Assagioli has demonstrated the myriad ways in which images and mental pictures tend to produce the physical conditions and external acts that correspond to them. An image or a thought in the mind fixes the same neural connections in the autonomic nervous system as the actual doing of it.

Jesus taught the same principle: Thinking and doing are no different. Lust is the same spiritual sin, Jesus said, as adultery. Hate is the same spiritual sin as murder (Matt. 5:21-28). The ultimate offender is not a body part but a spirit. If the inner ecology of our being is not kept clean, the outside will not be clean either. Everything we take in— air, food, images, smells—is food for our consciousness. We can pollute our spirits as well as pollute our soils and stomachs. Hence "whatsoever things are honest, true, just and lovely," Paul wrote from his prison cell, "think on these things" (Phil. 4:8 based on KJV).

> ## Sarvam-annam.
> ## (All is food.)
>
> *Indian saying*

If we meditate on the good, the true, and the beautiful, we become good and true and beautiful. Meditation is a biblical concept that is frequently mentioned in the Psalms. Two Hebrew words are used to translate the word "meditation." The first is *siach*, which means "to go over something in one's mind." What one goes over in one's mind, according to the psalmist, is God's words and works. "On thy wondrous works, I will meditate" (145:5 RSV); "I will meditate on thy precepts" (119:15 RSV). The second Hebrew word translated as "meditation" is *hagah,* which literally means giving voice to the "deepest longings of the heart and mind." Thus "Let the words of my mouth and the meditation *(hagah)* of my heart be acceptable in thy sight."[18]

The greatest killer in Western culture is heart disease. "It is from within, from the human heart, that evil intentions come" (Mark 7:21). Jesus measured morality in spiritual as much as physical terms.

The evidence accumulates with every passing study: Thoughts and beliefs can quickly become self-fulfilling prophecies—for ill or for well.

I

As one example of how "for ill" the mind affects the body, take the level of violence that is increasing in USAmerica. We live in a killing society. In the 1960s and '70s the most popular course at Amherst College was "Human Sexuality." The most popular course at Amherst in the 1990s—indeed, the most popular course in the school's entire history? "Murder."

USAmerican culture prefers tearing apart bodies to touching or titillating them.

Our urban areas are filled with "724 children." These "724" children are defined as kids placed by their parents in the protective custody of the home for seven-days-a-week, twenty-four-hours-a-day, with no outdoor playing or venturing into the streets without a beeper. USAmerican boys and girls are living in "lockdown" because of the horror zone of violence outside.[19] USAmerica, the most violent nation in the industrialized world, must begin to see preventive healthcare as encompassing preventing outbreaks of social diseases like violence as well as preventing outbreaks of old "social diseases" like venereal disease.

The Oliver Stone/Quentin Tarantino movie *Natural Born Killers* (1994) lays the violence of American society squarely at the feet of *Hard Copy, A Current Affair,* and *Inside Edition,* as well as with supermarket tabloids, local newscasts, news-magazines, and the long-term drip effect of the media's violent images on human thought patterns.

It simply won't do to say that the violence on the screen is but a mirror of a violent society. That's a profound half-truth. What's profound about its truth is that, first of all, the problem of violence is not a new one. Violence is not new to post-modern society. In England during the eighteenth and early nineteenth centuries, the most popular reading materials of the day were not sermons, but execution broadsheets. Capital convictions had risen so dramatically in the early nineteenth century that by the 1830s, over 90 percent of hangings were not carried out because there simply weren't enough scaffolds available to string up everyone given a capital conviction. Public hangings were not abolished until 1868 in England.[20]

Second, what's profound about this truth is that the problem of violence on the screen must not blind us to the problem of what is in the streets. Violence is the result of a number of interacting factors—genetic, perinatal, physiological, familial, environmental, economic, and theological.

Stephen King says the monsters are always there in their cages; what he does (along with Agatha Christie, Ernest Hemingway, William Faulkner, and a host of others) is take them for a walk every now and then. We must be careful not to pin violence on some cheap donkey-targets and easy scapegoats.

But while these things are profoundly true, they're not true enough. There's another half to the profound half-truth, and that half is the fact that violence on the screen is also a cause of violence in the streets. The visual consumption of violence is directly related to the virulent outbreaks of violence in the culture. In one evening news-broadcast, you see more violence than you will personally experience in a lifetime. This concentrated violence creates a climate of fear that helps escalate the level of violence and tragically shapes a culture of violence with more and more violent programming.

I'll never forget the impact on my life of the Russian roulette scene from *The Deer Hunter*. I harbored game fantasies after seeing this film that I had to bring under psychological subjection through spiritual warfare. It was not until 1988 that I realized I wasn't alone. In that year a study found that the number of railway suicides among West German boys aged fifteen to nineteen rose significantly after a television depiction of a teenager jumping under a train.

A pioneering study of the role of images in behavior formation was done in 1956. One dozen four-year-olds watching the violent "Woody Woodpecker" cartoons were compared with twelve preschoolers watching the irenic "Little Red Hen." They found that the "Woody Woodpecker" children were more prone to hit other children, verbally attack their classmates, break toys, and engage in disruptive, destructive behavior.

Since 1956 some three thousand studies of this issue (85 percent of them major research efforts) have revealed the same thing. Michael Medved reviewed one thousand studies conducted between 1960 and 1990, and found that 86 percent claimed a direct linkage between prolonged exposure to violence and higher levels of hostility and aggressiveness.[22] In another sampling of eighty-five major studies, only one failed to find a causal relationship between TV violence and actual violence. It was sponsored by NBC.

We have yet to study the impact of high technology toys that are teaching our children to use weapons to destroy

> **Hate is like acid. It can damage the vessel in which it is stored as well as destroy the object on which it is poured.**
>
> *Ann Landers* [21]

things rather than to use their imaginations to save the world. We probably don't need a study. We already know that children who watch more violent television are more aggressive than their peers who don't.

"There is more published research on this topic than on almost any other social issue of our time," University of Kansas Professor Aletha C. Huston, chair of the American Psychological Association's Task Force on Television and Society, told Congress in 1988. "Virtually all independent scholars agree that there is evidence that television can cause aggressive behavior."[23]

One longitudinal study of the viewing habits of children, conducted over a twenty-two-year period, found that the single best predictor of violent or aggressive behavior in adults, even more than economic, racial, or parental factors, is the consumption of violent images on television (action-adventure programs, cartoons, and so on). Likewise, other psychologists have worked with preschoolers and early school-age children to see if there are links between television viewing of aggression and overt aggressive behavior by children. Again, the correlation was so high it could not be ignored.

> *Our thoughts, if left to themselves, are a cage of unclean birds or a den of wild beasts.*
>
> *Charles Haddon Spurgeon*

Since one of this nation's biggest exports to the world is violent programs (whereas comedy differs from one culture to another, every country understands violence),[24] cross-cultural studies of the marketization of violence in five countries—Australia, Finland, Poland, Israel, and the U.S.—reveal that, in Rowell Huesmann's words,

once a script for aggressive behavior is stored, whether or not
it is ever retrieved may depend on whether it is rehearsed.
One form of rehearsal is daydreaming . . . greater aggressive
behavior and more TV violence viewing were associated with
more frequent aggressive and heroic daydreams in most
countries. . . . Violent TV (and violent behavior) may stimulate violent fantasies, and violent fantasies may increase the
likelihood of violent behavior.[25]

Childhood exposure to violent television content does not
even begin to address the reality of a children's culture in
which (in Los Angeles) 10 to 20 percent of homicides are witnessed by children, or in which (in New Orleans) 90 percent of
elementary school-age children have witnessed violence, 70
percent have seen a weapon used, and 40 percent have seen a
corpse.[26] This does not include the 3.3 million children in
America each year who witness their parents hitting, punch-
ing, slapping, or fatally assaulting each other with guns or
knives. One study argues that childhood exposure to television
is a "predisposing factor" in 50 percent of all violent acts.[27]

If true, this would mean, at least hypothetically, that
without television violence there would today be, according
to one researcher, "10,000 fewer homicides each year in the
United States, 70,000 fewer rapes, and 700,000 fewer injuri-
ous assaults."[28] Even if the argument is "Hey, it's only 4 to 6
percent of violence, not 50 percent, that can be accounted
for by media influence," my response is "Wow, that's a lot!"

In 1976 the American Medical Association House of Dele-
gates warned in a resolution on the eighteen thousand hours
of television kids watch by age eighteen that "TV violence
threatens the health and welfare of young Americans."[29] Now
the *Journal of the American Medical Association* reports that the
high gore content of television constitutes a "public health
problem" of almost epidemic proportions, creating a third
party in the cycle of violence: the victim, the criminal, and
the person who witnesses the violence. It recommends that
children's exposure to television violence should become
"part of the public health agenda, along with safety seats,

bicycle helmets, immunizations, and good nutrition."[30] The American Academy of Pediatrics is already on record with a policy statement: "Pediatricians should advise parents to limit their children's television viewing to 1 to 2 hours per day."[31]

The evidence is overwhelming and conclusive. Viewing violence from infancy to adulthood is positively correlated with acting out violent and aggressive behavior. No wonder USAmerica ranks with South Africa, the West Bank, and Cambodia as the most violent places to live on planet Earth. Four-letter images are more powerful than four-letter words. We have been taught that there are certain words one shouldn't say. We also at the very least should attach warning labels to violent material, and consider offering alternative, "family-friendly" newscasts in which violent images are sanitized.

> **We are what we think. All that we are arises with our thoughts. With our thoughts, we make our world.**
>
> *The Buddha*

No one wants to do anything to abridge freedom of expression. But if one's artistic "freedom" requires showing bodies getting killed or blown up, one ought to be made to "pay for it" in partial reimbursement for what society will ultimately have to pay for. Rather than a ban on made-for-TV murders, why not a tax of ten thousand dollars per corpse?[32]

Jesus' saying about the body's light needs to be stamped on the forehead of postmodern culture:

> The lamp of the body is the eye. If your eyes are sound, you will have a light for your whole body; if your eyes are bad, your whole body will be in darkness. If then the only light you have is darkness, how great a darkness that will be. (Matt. 6:22-23 REB; cf. Luke 11:34-36)

This version is from the Sermon on the Mount. The newly discovered dialogue-gospel, *The Dialogue of the Savior* 8, renders it: "The lamp of the body is the mind. As long as the things inside you are set in order . . . your bodies are luminous. As long as your hearts are dark, the luminosity you anticipate [is darkness]."[33]

II

As another example of how "for well" the mind affects the body, take the healing properties of the mind. Changes in thought patterns can awaken the inner healer and stimulate the immune system to protect itself against disease. Evidence of the links between the brain and the immune system can no longer be dismissed as so much New Age psychobabble.[34]

The *will* to be healed is as important as the wherewithal of healing. "Wilt thou be made whole?" was the paralyzing question Jesus asked the paralyzed man by the pool of Bethesda (John 5:6 KJV). For complete healing to take place, Jesus needed a partner (*synergos*). Part of the healing power of both physician and clergy resides in the belief and confidence of their patients and their parishioners.[35]

That is why some medieval commentators treated penance and anointing the sick as different aspects of a single sacrament. "Right" thoughts and "right" relationships furthered human growth into wholeness and holiness. One scholar has even argued that pain is not a sensation so much as it is a perception, a perception that comes freighted with the fears and hopes, the *ficta* and *facta*, of previous experience.[36]

The mind-body puzzle has not been solved, and in truth, explorations in

> **Many illnesses can be cured by one medicine: love and compassion.**
>
> *Tibetan saying*

cognitive consciousness (perceiving, remembering, reasoning) and sensory consciousness (feeling, acting) are but in their infancy. But already there seems to be a complex communication system that links the brain and the body.

This doesn't mean that every time you're sick you make yourself that way, nor does it mean that good thoughts will cure cancer. The AIDS crisis exposed the too-easy connection between mind and body that was touted by too many New Age-based self-healing spiritualities.[37] What it does mean is that your mental state, either positively or negatively, will affect your risk of developing disease and your response to treatment once an illness develops.

The "secondhand smoke" phenomenon demonstrates the ways in which we suffer the effects of what other people take into their bodies. But the same goes for the spiritual. In fact, some have already begun to talk about how each of us puts out "mood-smoke" that affects those who live around us.

There is a spiritual force field around each one of us that everybody has to deal with. We can emit a positive force field that inspires others, or a negative force field that enervates others. Affirming your physician has been shown to improve the precision of your diagnosis and the quality of your healthcare.[38]

This phenomenon of secondhand spiritual smoke is already being called "The Mother Teresa Effect." This is the technical name given to a Harvard study conducted by David McClelland that reports that when college students were given a film of Mother Teresa to look at, and they internalized images depicting her tending the sick and dying poor of Calcutta, their immune functioning (as measured by salivary immunoglobulin A concentrations) immediately increased and remained elevated one hour later. Merely *watching* compassion affects the observer positively.[39]

The biblical principle of the power of giving is this: "One who gives water will get water" (Prov. 11:25). Or in Jesus' own words, "Give, and it will be given to you" (Luke 6:38). We enrich ourselves by giving to others. The health benefits of giving freely and generously rebound powerfully on the giver, even if the persons doing the giving are themselves suffering from the worst diseases imaginable.[40] This is one reason Erich Fromm found poverty so degrading and debilitating: "It deprives the poor of the joy of giving." Jesus so blurred distinctions between self, other, and himself—"Inasmuch as you did it to one of the least of these . . . you did it to Me" (Matt. 25:40 NKJV)—that he promised that helping others would be experienced as helping Christ and helping oneself.[41]

People are literally making themselves sick. Every month new studies emerge that demonstrate the physiological effects of mental attitudes. PS^2 stands for Profound Sensitivity Syndrome,[42] an accessible way of describing a biochemical phenomenon in which faulty thought patterns ("cognitive distortions"), troubled emotions, hurtful feelings, and distorted ambitions create biochemical explosions in the body. The emerging field of psychoneuroimmunology (PNI) is exploring the way our immune systems are affected by our emotions.[43]

Jesus' conviction of a connection between mind and body went so far as to make explicit the linkages between anger and killing. "You have heard that it was said to those of ancient times, 'You shall not murder'; and 'whoever murders shall be liable to judgment.' But I say to you that if you are angry with a brother or sister, you will be liable to judgment" (Matt. 5:21-22). Interestingly, while some manuscripts include the phrase "without a cause," in the *Gospel of the Nazarenes* (the Jewish Gospel), the phrase is lacking.

We pay for our anger—physically and mentally. Emotions of fear and anger cause physical ailments. One Duke University research team found that people who slow-burn in anger have two to five times the death rate as do people with high blood pressure or people who smoke. Anger, hostility, jealousy, and depression conspire to shorten life, literally, as surely as high blood pressure, smoking, alcoholism, and so forth.

In their book *Anger Kills,* Redford B. Williams and Virginia Williams say that anger "is like taking a small dose of some slow-acting poison . . . every day of your life."[44] Anger is called a "toxic" emotion, especially unresolved anger that goes by the name of "hostility." Hostile people have one of the highest rates and risks of premature death.

Just revisiting angry moments in one's life can create abnormal heartbeats and electrical activity. Anger depresses the immune system. Anger can take a greater toll on the heart than

> *We think about our feelings and get migraine headaches;*
>
> *We swallow our feelings and get ulcers;*
>
> *We carry the weight of our feelings and get back pain;*
>
> *We sit on our feelings and get hemorrhoids.*
>
> *James Zullo* [45]

strenuous exercise or psychological stress.[46] According to Stanford psychiatrist C. Barr Taylor's research, anger can even bring on a heart attack in someone with severe heart disease.[47] Robert J. Stoller, psychiatrist and specialist in human sexual behavior (1924–1991) who died tragically in an auto accident and who taught in the School of Medicine at UCLA, said that "Perversion is the erotic form of hatred."[48]

This does not mean that expressions of anger or grief are harmful to emotional health. Jesus did not dwell on his negative emotions, but neither did he repress or deny them. Jesus was alive and at home with his emotions. Jesus vented his anger in constructive ways. Repressed anger leads to disease, depression, and even suicide.[49]

Jesus could be quite ornery at times, as his one-man raid

on the Jerusalem Temple revealed. Jesus also depicted a God who can become quite "judgmental" against those who refuse to love and forgive. " 'You scoundrel! I cancelled the whole of your debt . . . ought you not to have shown mercy to your fellow-servant just as I showed mercy to you?' And . . . he condemned the man to be tortured." Jesus warned, " 'That is how my heavenly Father will deal with you, unless you each forgive your brother from your hearts' " (Matt. 18:32-35 REB). "Anyone who nurses anger against his broth-

> *The great majority of us are required to live a life of constant, systematic duplicity. Your health is bound to be affected if, day after day, you say the opposite of what you feel, if you grovel before what you dislike and rejoice at what brings you nothing but misfortune. Our nervous system isn't just a fiction, it's a part of our physical body, and our soul exists in space inside us, like the teeth in our mouth. It can't be forever violated with impunity.*
>
> *Boris Pasternak*[50]

er must be brought to justice. Whoever calls his brother 'good for nothing' deserves the sentence of the court" (Matt. 5:22 REB).

And then, as if Jesus wanted to make sure these stern, severe words really sank in, he continued: "whoever calls him 'fool' deserves hell-fire." Jesus got very upset when people who professed to be in love with God lived at loggerheads with one another. Jesus taught that

> when you refuse to forgive, you kill the Messiah.
> when you refuse to love, you kill the Messiah.
> when you refuse to help, you kill the Messiah.

How many so-called Christians are in actuality part of the ageless conspiracy to kill the Messiah?

The 1993 American Heart Association study of the role of emotions in heart disease stopped short of naming emotions an independent risk factor in heart disease, but they made a strong case for considering emotional issues in heart disease prevention and treatment.[51] Jonathan Shedler, Professor of Clinical Psychology at the Institute of Advanced Psychological Studies at Adelphi University, announced to the 1992 meeting of the American Psychological Association that his studies revealed that suppressing anxiety and distress can mean a higher risk of heart disease. Another recent study by the Centers for Disease Control and Prevention in Atlanta shows that even at mild to moderate levels, depression can promote blood clots and thickening of the artery walls, wreaking cardiovascular havoc on the system.[52]

Various psychological factors are being found to promote diseases in almost every study of the linkages of mind and body. One study found that depressed men were more likely to develop cancer, and twice as likely to die of it.[53] A review article on the literature of "The Mind, the Body, and the Immune System" concludes: "the mind working through the immune system may tip the balance between health and illness in certain situations, possibly by way of stress hormones."[54]

Mental states can affect the course of a disease once it develops. Hope is the "sure enough" factor that makes a big difference in the outcome of disease. This headline appeared on the *USA Today* Life section (Section D) on 18 April 1994: "Pessimism Takes Toll on the Ill" with the first paragraph reading: "A highly pessimistic outlook shortens the lifespan of adults under 60 who suffer a recurrence of cancer, a new study suggests." There is healing power to hope and to the imagination that we have only begun to tap. I first learned the power of guided imagery when Coach Jack Kobuskie, my high-school basketball coach, told me to visualize the ball going into the hoop every time I stood at the free throw line. My shooting percentage increased dramatically (though still not enough to get me on first string). The percentages for survival increase dramatically for those using positive imagery to fight cancer cells, according to the pioneering research done by Carl and Stephanie Simonton, in Fort Worth, Texas.

> *Mind is by its very nature a singulare tantum. I should say: the overall number of minds is just one.*
>
> Erwin Schrödinger,
> Nobel physicist [55]

A ten-year study of women with metastatic breast cancer "stunned" researchers at Stanford University and the University of California at Berkeley. As reported to the American Psychiatric Association by Dr. David Spiegel, those patients with supportive communities around them, and those with positive mental attitudes toward their disease, often survived up to twice as long as a "control" group of patients. This study has been corroborated by Joseph G. Courtney of the University of California, Los Angeles, who reports that job-related stress increases the risk of colorectal cancer by 5.5 times, even after diet, exercise, and other preventatives have been factored out.[56] The liver appears especially vulnerable to stress-mediated cancers.

It is important not to get New Agey when discussing the externalization of mind. Bad thoughts don't cause cancer, and good thoughts don't cure cancer. What does happen, however, is that the thoughts and emotions we allow into our being have an effect on the immune system. Psychology affects physiology. And even when that effect may only be 5 to 10 percent—many factors influence disease, includ-

> ***Don't give up. There is a God somewhere. Deep calleth unto deep.***
>
> *Samuel Proctor*[57]

ing genes, food habits, and so forth—that 5 percent can be enough to awaken your immune system and start up your self-healing abilities (cut your finger with a razor, and it heals itself—that's the healing life force within each of us). Or put more dramatically, that 5 to 10 percent can mean the difference between living and dying.

Medical researcher and psychiatrist David Larson reviewed twelve years of psychiatric literature in the 1992 issue of the *American Journal of Psychiatry*. More than 90 percent of the studies showed a link between religion and good mental health. Religion proved to be protection against suicide, drug and alcohol abuse, and depression.[58] Similar findings come from other disciplines. Medical sociologist Kenneth F. Ferraro of Purdue University has discovered in his research that active participants in religious activities report significantly higher states of health and well-being than those who don't.[59] The correlation between the higher level of religious participation and the greater health of the participant, Purdue researchers hypothesize, is because religious people tend to avoid unhealthy excessive behavior, religious activity provides social support networks, and religion adds the vital element of hope to suffering.

Pick the greater predictor of getting a cold: Stop going to your church fellowship group or have a disaster happen at work.

Actually, it's the former.

Not doing regular pleasurable things (like getting together with friends) can be worse on the immune system

> ## As [a man] thinks in his heart, so is he.
>
> *A wise saying of Solomon (Prov. 23:7 NKJV)*

than negative developments. Psychologist Arthur Stone of the medical school at the State University of New York, Stony Brook, argues that positive events of the day seem to have a stronger and more helpful impact on immune function than upsetting events do a negative one.[60] Pleasant experiences such as worship and fellowship benefit the immune system for two days, some studies reveal, while negative events impair the immune system for one day. One of the ways Jesus got himself in mental shape was through music. Jesus sang praise hymns to God—even when times got tough. "When they had sung the hymn, they went out to the Mount of Olives" (Matt. 26:30; Mark 14:26).

The Last Supper (or what really should be called The First Supper) ended with a hymn.

But what kind of hymn? Most likely the Last Supper was celebrated as a Paschal meal. If so, the hymn would have probably been the second half of the passover *Hallel* (the Hebrew verb *halal* means "to praise"), praise psalms or Psalms 115–18.[61] In other words, the eucharistic meal ended with praise hymns, either all or parts of Psalms 115–18 (less probably Psalms 135–36). Before Jesus sweat blood literally in the Garden of Gethsemane over what he was to do next, he first sang praise songs.

The universe began with a big bang, say scientists, and the music of the first spheres continue to echo through creation to this day. Job says the universe began with music and laughter (God said: "When I laid the foundation of the earth . . . the morning stars sang together and all the heavenly beings shouted for joy" [Job 38:4, 7]).

Music is a creative force that can bring about spiritual, mental, and even physical change. Musicologist Deryck Cooke has demonstrated that certain melodic, harmonic, and rhythmic forms have deep connections with specific moods and emotions.[64] We are only beginning to appreciate the healing power of music, and the way different musical tones, rhythms, instruments, and arrangements work on different parts of the body. Worship, if it lifts up Christ, can put back "the missing tones" into our bodies, and prepare us for whatever the future might bring.[63]

It is amazing to see how medical people, many of them outside the Christian community, are singing the church's song about a God of medicines and miracles more ravishingly than the church itself. Medical missionary and surgeon Paul Brand, oncologist Bernie Siegel, Yale surgeon Richard Selzer, and Baltimore endocrinologist Neil Solomon are but a few of the medical names that are associated in the popular mind with the need for medicine to incorporate the spiritual. Solomon says that "nothing on this earth can produce in human beings the intensity of focused emotional impact for potential cure and healing than faith in God has been discovered to do."[64]

The director of international health at World Vision, Eric Ram, puts it like this:

> Whenever we offer acceptance, love, forgiveness, or a quiet word of hope, we offer health. When we share each other's burdens and joys, we become channels of healing. No matter how timid or tired, selfish or crazy, young or old, we all have something important to offer each other. Each of us is endowed by God with that gift of healing.[65]

Bernie Siegel was not the first to claim that "love heals" or that "unconditional love is the most powerful stimulant of the immune system."[66] Jesus taught that love, joy, hope, and forgiveness have physiological consequences in the same way despair and depression do. Jesus looked on life with eyes for what was best and soundest and noblest in people.

> ## A heart at peace
> ## gives life to the body.
> *(Prov. 14:30 NIV)*

In fact, Paul Brand calls Paul's "fruit of the Spirit"—Love, Joy, Peace, Patience, Gentleness, Goodness, Faithfulness, Humility, and Self-Control (based on Gal. 5:22-23)—a polyvalent vaccine for the prevention of almost all diseases that have behavioral bases.[67] Taken together, a fruit-of-the-Spirit elixir is the best health cocktail one can take.

III

Up to this point in exploring the mind, we have focused on thoughts. We have not even broached the subject of prayer, and we have used the word "prayer" only once. If mere thoughts are as powerful as we are suggesting, for good or ill, what about prayer?

Prayer is the most powerful force in the universe. Indeed, I have come to a place in my spiritual journey where I now think of prayer as a physical force that affects our universe in both seen and unseen ways. The most fundamental thing in the universe is spirit. Michael Talbot translates this into the language of physics: "Every cubic centimeter of empty space contains more energy than the total energy of all the matter in the known universe." Or put in other terms, the energy of a trillion atomic bombs is found in every cubic centimeter of space.[68]

We live in an ocean of energy—physical and spiritual. There is no more powerful spiritual energy than prayer. Indeed, prayer's power on the mind is measurable, just as measurable as the power of alcohol or drugs. That is why whatever we choose to pick up must be soaked in prayer—not prayer to ask God to bless what we are doing, but prayer to ask God to make what we do a part of what God is blessing.

In Mary Gordon's recent collection of three novellas, *The Rest of Life,* the book's title story contains this line: "There is some line running through her body like a wick." Prayer enabled Jesus' life to burn along this single wick: "I seek to do not my own will but the will of him who sent me" (John 5:30). It was through daily walking the path of prayer that Jesus stayed on track with the wick of truth.

There are twenty-one references to Jesus praying in the Gospels; this compares with sixteen times Jesus is said to have preached, and forty-five times Jesus is said to have taught.

Although Jesus only referred to his own prayer life once— what must it have been like for Peter to have heard our Lord tell him "I have prayed for you" (Luke 22:32)? Before every big moment, every big decision, every turning point, every crisis, Jesus prayed. Luke, the doctor of prayer, makes this clear: Before Jesus chose the twelve, he prayed (Luke 6:12); before his baptism, he prayed (Luke 3:21); before he challenged the disciples about whom he really was, he prayed (Luke 9:18); before the transfiguration, he prayed (Luke 9:29); before his arrest, he prayed (Luke 22:39-46); on the cross, he prayed (Luke 23:34); Jesus enters heaven on the wings of a prayer (Luke 23:46). Jesus' last words on planet Earth are a prayer of trust and hope, as he entrusted his final breaths into God's keeping: "Father, into your hands I commit my spirit" (REB).

But Jesus didn't just pray when he was desperate and in despair. He prayed without ceasing, constantly communing with God. Prayer was for Jesus a way of living—of the mind, body, and spirit being one. Jesus himself was a prayer. Jesus lived Psalm 109:4—"I am all prayer."[69] He so lived his life that prayer was not something he did with his lips but was something he did with his whole being. With every breath he took, Jesus lived a life of prayer. It is in this sense of literally becoming The Lord's Prayer that the monks have taught us "as long as you know you're praying, you're probably not."

But prayer was also something Jesus specifically did. He shut the door and prayed. "He went out to the mountain to pray" (Luke 6:12); "He went out to a deserted place, and there he prayed" (Mark 1:35); Jesus prayed all night; Jesus prayed alone (Luke 9:18-20); Jesus prayed for individuals (Luke 22:31), and for groups (Luke 23:34). How did Jesus calm the storm at sea and the storm in the souls of his disciples? He emerged from the mountaintop (Matt. 14:25) after having communed with God.

Prayer is the language of the soul. When one learns to live this language, the windows of heaven fling wide open. When Jesus prayed, things happened. When we pray, things will also happen. First, Jesus spoke as one having authority—"You are a teacher come from God" (John 3:2 NKJV). A daily diet of prayer anchors us to the eternal, and keeps our relationship with God fresh and clean. We must speak *to* God before we speak *for* God.

Second, he spoke as no one ever spoke before. When prayer breaks down the plaque build-up in our blood supply and lets the resurrection power flow freely through our bodies, there is such a release of power that it can give others what my West Virginia ancestor used to call "Holy Ghost goosebumps." Even though "we do not know how to pray as we ought," the promise is that the "Spirit interedes [for us] with sighs too deep for words" (Rom. 8:26).

Third, Jesus was able to wage spiritual warfare and he cast out devils. There is a well-known maxim of Ignatius of Loyola that says we are to pray as if everything depended on God, but to act as if everything depended on ourselves. There are some forces at work in our world that cannot be dealt with or cast out save by prayer.

Fourth, he healed the mind, body, and spirit, as well as a world sick in soul. Prayer keeps us whole. The physical and

> *Prayer is the test of everything;*
> *Prayer is also the source of every-*
> *thing;*
> *Prayer is the driving force of*
> *everything;*
> *Prayer is also the director of*
> *everything.*
> *If prayer is right, everything is*
> *right.*
> *For prayer will not allow anything*
> *to go wrong.*
>
> *Theophan the Recluse*
> *(1815–1894)* [70]

mental benefits of prayer are no longer seen by the medical community as superstitious nonsense. Physician Larry Dossey's work demonstrates that prayer has a positive impact on everything from high blood pressure to hemorrhoids. Bernie Siegel predicted in 1985 that meditation breaks will be as routine in our future as coffee breaks are today.

Finally, Jesus generated spiritual dynamics that connected others to the primal elements of the universe. Through prayer people are healed. Through prayer people are saved. Through prayer people become new. Through prayer we enter into the creative soul and Creator Soul of the universe. Every spiritual awakening in USAmerican history has begun as a prayer movement. In fact, we are right now in the vortex of a prayer awakening, what some are calling "the most significant prayer movement in the history of the church."

The power of prayer has never been stated more vividly than in these words of Jesus:

> And again I tell you: if two of you agree on earth about any request you have to make, that request will be granted by my heavenly Father. For where two or three meet together in my name, I am there among them. (Matt. 18:19-20 REB)[71]

Set the Table

J esus spoke the language of food. He used food to teach, heal, build community, transform village life, and break down walls of alienation and oppression.

Food was the language used by the social prophet named Jesus to subvert the wisdom of the world and to introduce people to the alternative wisdom of God and the ways of creation.[1] Indeed, the Jesus movement was a culinary revolution that invited people to "taste and see" the goodness of God. To eat all kinds of food, clean and unclean, was the daily expression of the theological revolution Jesus effected, whereby everybody became brothers and sisters in the new household of faith, even those who were previously declared "unclean": the disabled, Samaritans, women, publicans, half-breeds, minors, and sinners.[2]

In the Scriptures, Jesus is frequently eating "good food with bad people."[3] Jesus enjoyed eating and drinking. He was serious about food. It is striking the degree to which Jesus pays attention to food. Indeed, reading the Gospels is almost a gastronomic pleasure. I often get hungry when I read the Gospels. It is one meal after another.

Here's a little pop quiz. How many meals can you name in the Second Testament? Here are the ones I can remember:

- Feeding of the five thousand.
- Feeding of the four thousand.
- Wedding at Cana of Galilee.
- The Last Supper.
- Grilled fish on the shore.
- Meal with Zacchaeus.
- Peter's mother-in-law serving supper.
- Disciples chewing on husks of grain on the Sabbath.
- Martha cooking while Mary sat and chatted with Jesus.
- Jesus' instructions to feed Jairus's newly healed daughter.

Jesus' repetitive food images also come to mind—banquet, feast, living water, heaven as a banquet, "I am the vine," and "I am the bread of life."

The Second Testament is filled with stories about breakfasts on the beach, ceremonial meals, large outdoor picnics, potluck suppers, wedding receptions, grand banquets, intimate dining for three, and so on. Sometimes Jesus even cooked breakfast for his disciples. Luke and Acts are especially noted for the range of table settings and theology of food, from Simon's mother-in-law (Luke 4:39) to Levi's feast (Luke 5:29) to the feeding of the five thousand (Luke 9:12-17);[4] and in Acts from the breaking of bread by the first Christians (Acts 2:42, 46) to the deacons serving at table to the hospitality Lydia extended toward Paul (Acts 16:15).[5] One scholar shakes his head in amazement at how "The function of cooking breakfast for the absent fishing-fleet does not look masculine; and the scene would have been astonishing even in the case of one not recently dead and buried."[6] Truly, in the "breaking of the bread," their "eyes were opened" and they "recognized him" (Luke 24:35, 31).

Jesus loved to eat. Usually not by himself. He even gathered strangers around the table with him so he wouldn't have to eat alone. "Food's no good by yourself," my mother was fond of saying. "Jesus ate with people, and I like to eat with people." So she did.

Biblical banquets are symbolic. They tell us of a God of joy and celebration, a God of life and health, a God who offers us "soul food," the very "bread of heaven." Religious people in Jesus' day, like our own, linked pain and piety. How many times have you sat down to a meal served at a church, looked down at the plate handed you, and thought to yourself "Shall I eat this? . . . Or have I?"

> ### *I'm not like other people. I don't like pain. It hurts me.*
>
> *Daffy Duck*

Do you know of any clergy with the notion that everything one eats need not taste like chicken? Even when I am picking up the tab, what do my clergy colleagues order? Chicken. I, for one, have begun singing that refrain first authored by Dean Jonathan Swift after an endless circuit of lunches with rabbit (the eighteenth century's equivalent of chicken):

> For [chickens] young and [chickens] old,
> For [chickens] hot and [chickens] cold,
> For [chickens] tender, [chickens] tough,
> We thank thee, Lord, we've had enough.

The establishment got on Jesus' case not only because he and his disciples ate good food with bad people; he also spent too much time eating. He didn't fast enough. He didn't frown enough. "Good people" both fasted and feasted (Mark 2:18). The "best people" fasted, like John the Baptist whom some scholars suggest came out of the Essene community and may well have lived at Qumran.⁷ Jesus likely visited the Qumran community in his teens (it was but a two-hour walk from Jericho). The lure to become a second John the Baptist must have been immense. But Jesus rejected John's monastic lifestyle and broke "the tradition of the elders."

Jesus mystified his contemporaries because he and his disciples didn't eat only drab meals. They were not big on fasting. Some people called him a glutton and drunkard. Jesus kept reminding them that fasting wasn't appropriate for a wedding party. Feasting was. "Can you expect the bridegroom's friends to fast while the bridegroom is with them?" (Mark 2:19 REB). But they wouldn't listen. In a world where prestige and social status was everything, Jesus made "the admiration of others" (see Matt. 6:1-6, 16-18) nothing.

John the Baptist preached to sinners. Jesus the Christ supped with sinners. John the Baptist evangelized sinners. Jesus the Christ entertained sinners. Where John offered baptism, Jesus offered food and compassion to the wicked and the wretched of the earth. Jesus had a food ministry, especially to the dispossessed. He virtually formed a "Food Club" that offered both physical and spiritual food for every person who needed it. In the words of biblical scholar Dennis E. Smith, "for many scholars the theme of table fellowship with outcasts is primary and essential to any valid reconstruction of the historical Jesus."[8] Jesus' table manners, Norman Perrin believed, constituted the major reason why some sought to kill him.[10]

> **The first man in history to reach out and voluntarily touch lepers didn't die of leprosy. He died at the hands of religious leaders who wouldn't have touched a leper on a bet.**
>
> *Jimmy Allen*[9]

Food is the second feature of Jesus' ministry on which the entire confraternity of Second Testament exegetes agrees. If you doubt how important mealtime rituals can be, try breaking patterns by sitting at someone else's customary place and behaving like they behave. Anthropologists who specialize in eating habits contend that

- In all societies, both simple and complex, eating is the primary way of initiating and maintaining human relationships. . . . Once the anthropologist finds out where, when, and with whom the food is eaten, just about everything else can be inferred about the relations among the society's members. . . . To know what, when, how and where, and with whom people eat is to know the character of their society.[11]
- The social function of meals and the religious significance of the table, where much original research in the Jesus tradition has been directed, make the centrality to Jesus' ministry of meals and hospitality all the more evident. It was through the language of food ("who eats what with whom under which circumstances"[12]) that the Jewish people expressed their identity as a community and their belief in God. As an offshoot of Judaism, the disciples of Jesus transformed the language of Second Temple Judaism about food in order to distinguish its identity and beliefs.[13]

Jesus drew some of his most striking parables from experiences he had at dinner parties. In fact, the last supper he shared with his closest friends the final night before his execution was in the form of a memorial meal. Jesus chose the context of a plain and simple meal as the one ritual path in which he was to be found.

For Jesus, the breeding was in the feeding. Jesus taught that God is present and becomes known more at table than in stone temples or on stone tablets. We encounter Christ not just in a specific holy meal but in every meal where people break bread with one another. Churches who have put together "Food Banks" and "Food Clubs" (contribute ten dollars per month so the church can buy food for people who need it) have understood that Jesus' teaching ministry cannot be separated from his food ministry.

Sometimes Jesus is a host. Sometimes a guest. Sometimes a servant. Sometimes a chef. Sometimes Jesus dined with the rich, sometimes with the poor. Sometimes Jesus dined with the "righteous," other times with "sinners." Mostly Jesus dined with the blind, lame, lepers, deaf, poor, widows, orphans, and hungry. But with whomever Jesus dined, that dinner became a messianic banquet of revolutionary consequences.

Jesus made himself known in the breaking of the bread. Jesus continues to make himself known to postmodern disciples in the baking and breaking of bread. The ability to make a good loaf of bread becomes almost a theological obligation, a religious ritual, a matter of spiritual hygiene. If we are to run together in faith, and stand together in truth, we must first kneel together in prayer, and sit together in food. With Christ.

Have you "set the table" for communion with God? for communion with others? for communion with yourself? When we "set the table" for communion with God, we can count on something magical happening. In a world where family

> **What are we to receive? A kingdom. For doing what? "I was hungry and you fed me." What is more ordinary, more of this world, than to feed the hungry, and yet it rates the Kingdom of Heaven.**
>
> *Augustine*

feuding has become a mealtime blood sport, Christ brings something special to the table. In fact, whenever Christ eats with us, there is transfiguration.

When Jesus dined with Zacchaeus, this chief tax collector's whole attitude toward life changed as Jesus came into his heart (Luke 19:1-10).

When Jesus dined with Levi (also known as Matthew), this tax collector learned that Jesus came not to bring in the royalty and "beautiful" people but he came to bring in the rogues and the sheaves, the robbers and the lowlifes like himself (Luke 5:31-32; Matt. 9:9-13).

When Jesus dined with Simon the Pharisee, Simon discovered why the lightweight fare of his life sat so heavily in his soul's stomach, and he learned that we can give all we've got to God only because God first gave it all for us (Luke 7:36-50).

When Jesus dined with his disciples, the disciples saw like never before how each of them could become great—by becoming servants and waiting at tables (John 13:1-20).

When Jesus ate dinner with the two disciples in Emmaus, the disciples' "eyes were opened" and they saw Jesus like they had never seen him before (Luke 24:31).

When Jesus dined with Lazarus, Mary, and Martha, they found a friend who sticks closer than a brother (John 12:1-8).

When Jesus dined with a sinful woman (possibly Mary Magdalene), she heard words of forgiveness and love she had never heard before and would never forget (Luke 7:36-50).

When Jesus cooked breakfast for Simon Peter and the disciples, Peter learned to look himself in the mirror without blinking (John 21:1-19).

When is the last time you let Jesus dine with you?

When you do, what will you serve?

I

Or will you dine out? What about takeout?

I don't think so. Not for Jesus. Not even for friends. The so-called "Betty Crocker effect" is over. "Natural" and "home-made" are now labels of distinction, not inferiority. Betty

Crocker taught our parents and grandparents that home-made goods are inferior and inefficient. Store-bought bread, store-ground coffee, store-canned vegetables—all were advertised as more nutritious and dependable than "homemade" goods. See something good? It's "the next best thing since sliced bread." Now people don't want sliced-bread—those mass-produced, standard-size, uniform-looking, bleached-white slabs of cardboard air. My guess is you will serve a bread that can be broken, a bread that flakes and crumbles.

This is a good time to be a fruit or vegetable. "Eat your vegetables" is not something parents need to say anymore. Everyone else is now saying it for them. "Eat More Plants" (vegetables, fruits, legumes, grains) has become the number one rule of healthy diets.

The only question among experts is whether to eat anything else *besides* plants. Perhaps your menu for Jesus will be filled with vegi ventures, even introducing some of planet Earth's best fruits most people have yet to know even exist—for example, premier fruits of the earth like lulos (the golden fruit of the Andes), mamones, rambutans, durians, and mangosteens. Perhaps your meal will begin and end with fruit soup and sorbet.

But will you serve Jesus meat? What about wine? What kind of butter will Jesus find in the butter dish? And will you make bread out of lard?

Husband and wife team Robert McKenzie and Marilyn Chilcote have started an electronic meeting on Ecunet entitled "Spirituality and Ethics of Eating." It quickly became one of the most hotly debated bulletin boards, and has made me wonder whether those who are calling food abuse "the last religious taboo"[14] might not be right.

While half of Americans routinely thank God before meals, it is easier for these same people to talk about their sex habits than their food habits. Studies have shown that women are more prone to discuss sex abuse and child abuse than food abuse. Yet on an average day sixty-five million Americans are dieting. This includes from 50 to 80 percent of fourth-grade girls, and two-thirds of high school students.[15] As many as one-third of female college students use laxatives, vomiting,

A Grace for Dieters

Are there graces for lettuce, Lord? And low-fat, meat-free, fun-free meals? I need you to send me words for blessing this paltry meal before me, Lord, for it is difficult to feel grateful for these skimpy portions when all I think of are the foods not on my plate. Help me change that thought, to make peace with choosing not to eat them, for I need help in becoming the healthier person I want to be. Hold up for me a mirror of the new creation you see me to be, for I need a companion at this table, Lord.

Margaret Anne Huffman[16]

and diuretics to purge their bodies. In light of Jesus' command
to "Eat . . . remembering me" (based on 1 Cor. 11:24 CEV),
McKenzie and Chilcote are asking an important question:
What does it mean to "eat remembering Jesus"?

Most religions have dietary restrictions and regulations
for health purposes. Most religions also have virtually abandoned their ethics of diet at the very time it is routine to
pick up health newsletters that feature articles on "Cancer-
Fighting Vegetables," "You Decide Your Age," "Foodaceuti-
cals (Food Drugs)," "Healing Foods," or "Mood Food" along
with daily newspapers that detail the worldwide progression
of reproductive disorders (including male infertility), degen-
erative respiratory conditions (asthma and chronic bronchitis), and immune deficiencies and decompositions.

Dietary measures have tremendous consequence on health.
In fact, the theme of John 6:51-58 might be known as "You Are
What You Eat." How we feel may also be mightily affected by
what we eat. Carrie Wiatt's book, *Eating by Design* (1995), argues
that one of the best ways to beat stress is through diet. Spinach,
okra, and kale can stave off bouts of minor depression.

As we have already seen in chapter 4, chronological age
and biological age can have very little correspondence. About
30 percent of aging is due to heredity. The rest is lifestyle—
mainly exercise and diet. Diet has been shown to alter cancer
cells, and even more significantly, to foster the production of
less metastatic cells.[17]

A lot of people are dying early deaths, killed by their own
hands, if forks and spoons
be allowed as weapons.

As I learned from the electronic bulletin board, it is
hotly contested by some
whether Jesus killed animals
for flesh or fur.[18] Some see
Jesus acquiescing in traditional Jewish practices (Matt.
11:18-19; Luke 22:15; 24:42-
43; John 21:9-13), and even

> *Let food be thy*
> *medicine and thy*
> *medicine food.*
>
> *Hippocrates*

abolishing restrictions ("Thus he declared all foods clean." Mark 7:19). Others argue that the King James Version, and many translations thereafter, chose the word "meat" to translate the generic "food." At the beginning of his public ministry, Jesus announced that his "meat" was to do the will of the One who had sent him (John 4:34). In the same spirit Paul announced that if eating meat would cause his brother or sister to stumble, he would refrain from flesh foods for as long as the world stands (1 Cor. 8:13; Rom. 14:20-21).

The question of how, in our patterns of eating, we honor our spiritual connections with creation is becoming more pressing and vital. In a world of fast foods, the church may consider starting its own version of the worldwide "slow-food" movement that is dedicated to prolonged and sensual enjoyment of food. It was founded by food-and-wine writer Carlo Petrini and his fellow members of Arcigola, an Italian gastronomical society. It goes by the name of the International Movement for the Defense of and the Right to Pleasure, and it issued in 1989 a "Slow Food Manifesto" that served as an opening salvo in the Slow Food Wars.

What is also clear is that the biblical support for the view that those who love animals shouldn't eat them becomes clearer every year. In the original creation and innocence of the Garden of Eden, all earthlings, human and animal, were vegetarians (Gen. 1:29-30). After the Fall, Adam and Eve's diet expanded from nuts, grains, and fruit to include whole plants and bread (Gen. 3:18-19). Only after the Flood did creation become carnivorous and humans eat flesh food.

Even then, however, there were instituted severe prohibitions against eating certain portions of flesh (Lev. 3:17; 7:22-27) which, if followed strictly, would have greatly

> **Der Mensch ist was er isst.**
> **(Man is what he eats.)**
>
> *Ludwig Feuerbach*

limited if not prohibited the eating of flesh entirely.[19] The whole kosher system works to penalize those who eat meat. If you're going to eat meat in the Jewish tradition, then you're going to have to take into consideration a lot of details. If you're vegetarian, you don't worry about anything. Kosher makes Judaism user-friendly to vegetarians, but not to carnivores.

Since the covenant with Noah (Gen. 9:2-3) and the Law of Moses (Deut. 12:15) gave biblical license for eating flesh, vegetarianism in Jewish and Christian history has been a minority practice (although its current popularity is increasing, with 12,750,000 USAmericans who consider themselves vegetarian, 1,657,500 of whom don't eat any meat, fowl, or fish). Throughout history, ascetics (the quasi-Essene community in Egypt known as the Therapeutae), those committed to nonviolence (see Philo's and Pythagoras's evaluation of meat-eating as an unnecessary form of violence because it involved bloodshed and butchering), and those in idolatrous environments—refused flesh food. The Bible's best known vegetarian, the prophet Daniel, proposes that a simple diet of vegetables would work even better than the king's diet of sweetmeats: "But Daniel made up his mind that he would not defile himself with the king's choice food or with the wine which he drank; so he sought permission from the commander of the officials that he might not defile himself" (Dan. 1:8 NASB).

[All 40 year olds] . . . listen up. Facts are that the warranty on you ran out about three years ago, parts are irreplaceable, and mechanics cost about $3,000 per hour.[20]

The Bible is also clear that when all things shall be ultimately reconciled to God, all carnivores shall become vegetarians, and a gentler, nonviolent way of living on the earth will be the norm. This was the text from Isaiah that caused the change in John Wesley's dietary habits toward a more vegetarian ideal:

> The wolf also shall dwell
>   with the lamb,
> The leopard shall lie down
>   with the young goat,
> The calf and the young lion
>   and the fatling together;
> And a little child shall lead them.
> The cow and the bear shall graze;
> Their young ones shall lie down
>   together;
> And the lion shall eat straw like the ox. . . .
> They shall not hurt nor destroy in all
>   My holy mountain,
> For the earth shall be full of the
>   knowledge of the LORD
> As the waters cover the sea. (Isa. 11:6-7, 9 NKJV)[21]

Later in Isaiah, the killing of animals is equated with murder: "Whoever slaughters an ox is like one who kills a human being" (Isa. 66:3).[22]

Whereas at first examination it appears that John the Baptist did not exclude locusts from his simple diet (Mark 1:6), upon closer scrutiny some scholars contend that John the Baptist's eating of grasshoppers and drinking of honey was an idiomatic way of saying he was a vegetarian and teetotaler, for these were Jewish substitutes for flesh and wine. The *artos* in Luke 7:33 stands for the Hebrew *lhm*, which in this case means flesh, not bread. The early Christian community ate meat, but meat-eating was confined to the lower-economic classes mainly at public festivals in the context of religious ritual. Eating flesh was not proscribed; but it was taken very seriously.

II

So now where are we? Would you serve Jesus meat or wouldn't you? It isn't an easy question to answer.

There are as many environmental, economic, medical, and moral reasons for vegetarianism as there are religious reasons. From an environmental standpoint, one of the worst uses of land is for grazing cattle. In fact, cattle-raising is one of the prime factors in the worldwide destruction of the rain forests. In South America, 38 percent of the Amazon forest has done been cleared for ranching. In Central America, more than 25 percent of the forests have been razed to make cattle pastures just since 1960. In western USAmerica, as much as 85 percent of the rangeland is being crushed to death, mostly by overgrazing.[23] In his study of the role of water in the West, Marc Reisner has shown how California consumes 5,214 gallons of water to produce one edible pound of beef as compared to 23 gallons of water for one pound of tomatoes. Reisner is offended that in California, more than three times the amount of water is used in raising cows than is consumed by people.[24]

From an economic standpoint, the issue is not only the sacrifice of animals to satisfy our appetites, but also the sacrifice of other human beings. The meat from one cow can nourish ten people for a certain period of time; the grain used to feed and fatten that cow for market could nourish for the same time period one hundred people.[25] The energy used to produce one pound of grain-fed beef is equal to one gallon of gasoline.

Flesh food can be seen as but another component of our massive institutionalization of gluttony, waste, and greed. One author who has analyzed a "60 Minutes" report based on statistics from the U.S. Department of Agriculture and the American National Cattlemen's Association—statistics that reveal that if we would grain feed our beef only ten fewer days we could save enough grain to preserve the lives of all the starving people of the world—makes this startling conclusion: "the grain we feed our meat animals is kept—figuratively, at least—off the plates of starving people around the world."[26]

From a medical standpoint, the Standard American Diet (SAD) is just what it says it is—a SAD diet that is encouraged by all these "All U Can Eat" come-ons. We eat too much, especially too much meat. Eating habits in the future will change—away from three "full-course meals" to five "snacks"—"daystart," "pulsebreak," "humpmunch," "hold-meal," and "evesnack."

It is true: The branch of biomedicine most filled with contradictory advice, hasty conclusions, and gullible customers, is nutrition. But it is also true that what we do eat is often unhealthy, a fact that has launched many quests for the "oily grail" (fat-free fried foods). The "Seeds of Change" movement is based on the philosophy that a plant-based diet best improves individual health and limits the impact of humans on planet Earth's resources.[27] Paul Theroux's novel *Millroy the Magician* starts with the protagonist (a preacher) asking "How can you take any religion seriously if it leaves out nutrition?"[28] The preacher is on a mission to cleanse our diet of fats and sugars and wean the U.S. from its "weenie worship" (love affair with the hot dog). He evangelizes a loaves and fishes diet from his nutritional guidebook, the Bible: "The book of life. The book of food. The book of meals and miracles."[29]

Seventh-Day Adventists, who refrain from meat, tobacco, or alcohol, live, on average, seven years longer than others and have one-seventh the heart attack rate. We know that for every pound you are over the proper weight for your size, you die, on average, one month prematurely. Fat-laden diets are chief contributors to colon cancer, heart disease, and help explain the high rates of breast cancer in Western countries.[30] The National Cancer Institute has a "designer foods" program that is attempting to find which

> ## *Eternity gives way to a salted cucumber.*
> *Russian proverb*

vegetables, fruits, herbs, and spices pack the heftiest anti-cancer punch.

Even if cutting back on fat in one's diet doesn't prevent cancer, as some argue, it may help diminish the chance of the cancer from becoming life-threatening. Fats may accelerate cancer even if they are proven not to cause cancer. Worldwide, up to half of all men over fifty have tiny, latent prostate tumors.[31] The more fiber and less fat in one's diet, the less chance one has of cancer becoming aggressive. Swedish investigators have concluded that dietary fat directly influences the growth of existing breast tumors, and low-fat diets may help women avoid recurrence of this disease that kills more than forty-six thousand women in the United States alone each year.[32]

The environmental, economic, and medical cases for vegetarianism, however, do not preempt the religious arguments. Far from vegetarians being "oddballs" and "weirdos," out of love for God and God's creation some are choosing not to eat meat as a sacrifice of praise. Andrew Linzey makes a powerful case for the fact that, while it may have been necessary for Jesus to eat fish in first-century Palestine, killing is not essential for human survival today. When it is possible to live without killing, it is right so to do. Thus Christian vegetarians "can rightly claim to be living closer to the biblical vision of peaceableness than their carnivorous colleagues."[33]

Indeed, it may well be that our descendants will see our wanton eating of flesh food, as decidedly sub-Christian as the patterns of eating that characterized some of our forebears. According to an Oxford don researching eating habits of monastic life, the Benedictine brothers at the Westminster Abbey around 1500 had a food and drink ratio that on some days totaled more than 7,375 calories. Considering the fact that men were much shorter then than now, and that the monastic life was quite sedentary, this was quite an adequate caloric intake. The diet included three pounds of meat a day plus a gallon of ale—supplemented on feast days with a bottle of wine. Thus, on an average day, almost 20 percent of a monk's total calorie intake was pure ethanol.[34]

Others argue that our descendants will deem our slaughter

of animals as decidedly sub-Christian as the holding of slaves or the silencing of women. They make a strong case. Clearly there is biblical permission for eating meat (see Gen. 9:3-4; Rom. 14:2-3; and 1 Tim. 4:3-4), but only in the same way there is biblical permission for holding slaves. The ideal of a world where there is neither slave nor free, the ideal of a world where the lion lies down with the lamb, lays the basis for the abolition of slavery and the abolition of flesh food. Just as animal sacrifice ended with the sacrifice of the Lamb of God, meat eating that was permitted (even commanded) before Christ's coming could now be seen as no longer necessary.

> **Man is the only animal that can remain on friendly terms with the victims he intends to eat until he eats them.**
>
> *Henny Youngman*

In sum, at the very least: Those Christians who argue the case against predatory lifestyles should not be made to feel odd or offbeat.

III

Yet the practice of flesh-eating will no doubt continue, and should. Yahweh was the first to make garments of skin to clothe Adam and Eve (Gen. 3:21). Although there is no direct evidence of Jesus himself eating meat, the Lord's Supper most probably was a Passover meal that consisted of all types of food—bread, vegetables, meat, fish, fruits, and drink. Jesus helped his friends catch fish to sell at market (Luke 5:4-7), the resurrected Jesus ate *broiled* (not fried) fish while his disciples watched (Luke 24:43), and Jesus prepared and served fish to his disciples (John 21:9).

Furthermore, as W. H. Drummond points out, while vegetarianism might be possible "in tropical regions abounding in esculent roots and vegetables," a vegetarian diet is unlikely in "regions of perpetual sterility" like the "Greenlanders and Esquimaux" must survive on.[35] Quaker naturalist Jim Corbett confesses "I slaughter animals, eat meat, and seek to live nonviolently."[36] A vegetarian world can be a very violent and violating one, as people like Hitler have proved over and over again in history. Apart from any consideration of eating habits, the Industrial Era may prove to be the most violent way of life ever invented.

But if one continues to eat flesh, certain things are important.

First, grace before meals becomes an absolute necessity. Whenever we sit down to a meal, remember that another earthling had to suffer or give up its life for our sustenance, and often under unspeakable conditions. The animal that one is now eating "had its throat slit, . . . has been reared and died in pain, . . . has been hung upside down and bled." Animals know when they are going to die. Slaughterhouse attendants testify that almost all pigs, forced up the ramp to the killing room, do one thing—they scream.

An animal was killed that we might eat that Big Mac. The least we can do is offer thanks for the gift of that life. We must acknowledge the common creaturehood of all sentient life, and show respect for these creatures that share life as we do.

Second, for health's sake some of us should consider limiting eating anything with a face to special days of celebration or commemoration. Whatever one's diet, there needs to be a leaning toward leanness. Many of us for health's sake need to dramatically reduce the nearly half a pound per day of red meat we consume. We also could change our eating habits for health's sake. The last of Bob Schwartz's four rules for going off diets (which also can apply to going off budgets, but that's another book) is the most important: 1) Eat when you're hungry; 2) Eat exactly what your body wants; 3) Eat each bite consciously; 4) Stop when your body has had enough.[37]

Third, until we have "smart" refrigerators that will monitor our "intake" like "smart" toilets will one day monitor our "outtake," lots of vitamins ("vital amines" is what they were originally called) and roughage should be taken to ward off the effects of a diet rich in flesh foods, whose fats promote cancer. The U.S. Department of Health and Human Services estimates that as much as 35 percent of all cancer deaths may be related to the foods we eat as part of our lifetime consumption of forty tons of food.

> *The average Westerner will eat twenty cows, fourteen hundred chickens, twelve pigs and thirteen sheep in his or her lifetime. That is a lot of lives.*
>
> Paul and Linda McCartney [38]

Those who eat meat need fruits and vegetables rich in antioxidants (that is, the vegetables that are dark green, orange, and yellow). Cruciferous vegetables (cabbage, broccoli, brussels sprouts, and cauliflower) are key components in a carnivorous, anti-cancer diet. People who eat the most fruits and vegetables have at least half the cancer rates of those who eat the least. Some studies reveal that our risk of stroke can be reduced by almost 70 percent by eating five servings of fruits and vegetables a day.

Small changes in lifestyle and eating habits can have big consequences. Mountains are moved one rock at a time. Even small doses of antioxidant vitamins C and E, when taken with beta-carotene, can boost immune function and reduce the risk of cancer and heart disease. One UCLA study found that men who take vitamin C daily live an average of six years longer. The church, through programs such as food banks and soup kitchens, can help people who can't afford it get daily doses of 15-20 milligrams of beta-carotene, 100-4,000 immunizing units (IUs) of vitamin E, and 250-1,000 milligrams of vitamin C. About 90 percent of USAmericans do not get this much through diet.

IV

A woman died and went to heaven. It was more beautiful than she'd ever imagined. She couldn't wait to show it to her husband (when he eventually arrived) because he was an eternal pessimist who made Murphy (of "Murphy's Law" fame) look like an optimist.

A year later her husband joined her and she took him on a tour. "The sky, the flowers, the music, the animals, the people—heaven is truly heaven, isn't it?" she exclaimed.

He surveyed Paradise briefly, then said, "Sure. And if it weren't for you and your doggoned oat bran, we'd have been here five years sooner."

I like to tell this story because it provides a healthy corrective to the Manichean heresy of "healthism," as expressed memorably by one cardiac specialist who gave a heart patient this new commandment of eating: "If it tastes good, spit it out." Want to bring great passions to the fore? Talk about sex, sin, and saturated fat. We have become a generation terrorized and traumatized by food. We are becoming a nation of food fetishists.

A cartoon in the *New Yorker* showed an executive in a suit and tie, standing behind his wife at the breakfast table and saying: "I feel like pushing the envelope this morning, honey, starting with a little grape jelly for that bran muffin." Whenever someone hesitates to embark on a recipe that reads like a pleasant invitation to suicide, I prescribe for them this bit of doggerel by some anonymous wit who memorably captures the biblical perspective:

Methuselah ate what he found on his plate,
And never, as people do now,
Did he note the amount of calorie count;
He ate it because it was chow.

He wasn't disturbed as at dinner he sat,
Devouring a roast or a pie,
To think it was lacking in granular fat
Or a couple of vitamins shy.

He cheerfully chewed each species of food,
Unmindful of troubles or fears,
Lest his health might be hurt
By some fancy dessert;
And he lived over 900 years.

Theologian Robert Farror Capon provides a needed corrective to the ideologies of "healthism" and vegan vigilantism. He helps us see that food is not our enemy. The fanatics will tell you that butter causes cancer, or that salt raises your blood pressure, or that eggs clog your veins. But eggs plus salt plus butter equal hollandaise, which rivals the computer chip in terms of satisfaction.

For some people, however, hollandaise sauce is, if not "sudden death," at least slow death. The Egyptians who tried to follow the Israelites through the parted waters learned the hard way what some of us are still learning the hard way: Not everything other people can do I can do. Not everything other people can eat or drink, I can eat or drink. What is life to you, is sometimes death to me. Some people can plead the cause "Bring Back the Glory That Was Grease." Others put on pounds just stirring the stuff.

The story goes that a young student came to a great preacher and asked, with a trembling voice, "Can Christians dance?" The preacher replied with great sobriety, and piety, "Some can, some can't." First Corinthians 10 insists that everything is permissible but asserts that not everything is constructive.

I, for one, have had enough of those self-righteous, card-carrying members of the "Look How Good I Am Because of

What I Eat Club." Unsanctified thoughts ran rampant when I learned that the health columnist for the *New York Post,* Stuart Berger, author of best-selling diet and health books that promised increased longevity to those who would follow his regimen,[39] died in 1994 at age forty. He weighed 365 pounds at the time of his death.

An ethical climate of moral vegetarianism is making "sinners" out of all hamburger-lovers. A mistyped bulletin once invited the congregation to sing the hymn "Come, Christians, Join to Sin." One parishioner replied to his vegetarian pastor, "Preacher, we're doing our best. We're doing our best." Even though it is not my idea of a good time to drape a dead deer over the fender each fall, it has become all too easy to take potshots at those like my brother who do. In the face of a growing vegetarian fundamentalism, the biblical all-may/none-must/some-should approach to meat must be heard. The herbivore left can scarcely claim moral superiority to the red-meat right.

Jesus exhibited a theology of enoughness, and envisioned a world where everyone has enough. Jesus himself knew what it meant to "Live *Dayenu.*" *Dayenu* is Hebrew for "It is enough." He lived simply and mindfully, and knew when "enough" was "enough" in his life.

> **He who knows he has enough is rich.**
>
> *Tao Te Ching*

Jesus lived a life of enoughness instead of too-muchness. In the words of the proverbialist, "Give me neither poverty nor wealth," but only enough (Prov. 30:8 NEB). Disciples of Jesus eat good food with bad people, and "Live *Dayenu.*"

CHAPTER SEVEN

Adopt a See-You-at-the-Party Spirit

* * *

Mission statements should be short and sharp.

San Francisco's Esprit de Corp gathered its employees together and they came up with three simple lines about the kind of business they wanted to be: "Be informed. Be involved. Make a difference."

Nike overheard people talking and let them name their three word mission statement: "Just do it."

Disney's three word mission statement trains thirteen thousand new employees each year. Every employee is required to live this mission as expressed in the child-speak of Disney: "Provide People Happiness."

Jesus of Nazareth has an equally short mission statement.

It is found most succinctly in the Gospel of John. The ancient church portrays each of the four Gospels with symbols that have often been carved into pulpits and placed in stained glass. The symbol for Matthew is the lion. Mark's symbol is a man. Luke's is an ox. The author of the fourth Gospel, John, is symbolized by the "eagle."

Why the high-flying eagle? Because of John's life-soaring, God-seeing faith. Alone in the animal kingdom, it is said, the eagle can look directly into the sun and not be blinded. Some have argued the word "eagle" comes from the Greek *aigle* meaning "brightness," "clarity," "torchlike brilliance." Nowhere in the Gospels is life so afire and affirmed as in John.

In fact, John 1:3-4 is as well translated by ending the first sentence after "anything made" rather than the more familiar "All things were made through Him, and without Him nothing was made *that was made* [emphasis added]. In Him was life" (NKJV). In this alternative and better translation, verses 3-4 should read "All things were made by him; and without him was not anything made." Then, as if someone suddenly asked what were these "all things" made by God, John responds: "What was made in him," he emphasizes, "was life."[1]

But what kind of "life"? If we continue on the eagle's path until the tenth chapter, the second half of the tenth verse, we find the answer. Here lies the mission statement of Jesus of Nazareth, and one of his greatest prescriptions for a healthy life. Not surprisingly, this verse was chosen as the theme for the Eighth World Youth Day (12-15 August 1993) when two hundred thousand pilgrims from seventy-five countries descended on Denver for Pope John Paul II's third U.S. visit.

> *If I keep a green bough in my heart, the singing bird will come.*
>
> Chinese proverb

Jesus' mission statement is this: "I came that they may have life, and have it abundantly."

Another translation puts it like this: "I have come . . . that you might have life—life in all its fullness" (GNB). Or in my personal translation, "I have come that you might *live it up.*" Since in John's Gospel the Greek words that speak of eternal life mean most fundamentally "life-plus," this verse could also be translated "I have come that you might have life-plus."

Jesus comes not so that we might have "my so-called life," as the hit baby buster television show sarcastically put it. Nor did Jesus come that we might have a "so-so," bland mediocre life, or an "artificial life." Jesus came to show us the way to a healthy, hyper-real, Spirit-filled, life-plus life. The Word made flesh to the full came to make all flesh full of the Word.

What kind of "life" is a healthy life? It is life full. Life abundant. Life full-grown. Life complete. Life plus. Life "perfect" (*teleios* means whole, complete, full-grown). Jesus offers us whole life. Not half life. Not term life. But full life. Life lived to its limits.

"Live it up" is not something disciples of Christ do for a weekend. "Live it up" is something we do for a lifetime. Living should not be a liability within a church founded by our Lord. Our mission is to help others come fully alive to the life God has given them, and to live that life up to its healthiest and fullest. In Pauline theology Christ is "fullness" (*pleroma*). In Hebrews Jesus is the "pioneer and perfecter of our faith" (Heb. 12:2). Jesus came that we might be full of it—full of life, full of the Spirit, full of aliveness, full of love, full of health.

"Live it up" is less a motto of self-fulfillment than of self-transcendence. One of the most amazing and mysterious things about Jesus is that his excess of life was so great that he was able "to lay it down for his friends" (compare John 10:11-18; 15:12-13; 1 John 3:16). To "live it up" in Jesus' sense of the word means "it" is God more than self. The highest goal in life, the highest good on earth, is not "to feel good about oneself." To "live it up" is to know Christ and to make Christ known. Or as Paul put it, "For to me, to live is Christ" (Phil. 1:21 NKJV). To "live it up" is to live a whole, healthy life.

With the mission statement of an eagle, why can't the church make Jesus Christ as magical and mysterious as Disney makes a mouse? Besides, what do eagles make of mice? Isn't it time to bring the magic back again? Isn't it time to restore to the church the sound of the snap, crackle, and pop of the Spirit? Christians don't need to sprinkle people with pixie dust so they can fly. We already have been sprinkled with the waters of baptism, which enable us to live a high-flying life.

It's time to be blunt. For many people what's problematic is not the reality of God in the world, but the reality of God in the church. C. S. Lewis's dictum that it is more difficult to convert the bored than the wicked is coming true right before our very eyes. How many people in old-line "church culture" do you know who leave

> *God threatens terrible things, if we will not be happy.*
>
> Jeremy Taylor[2]

home for worship with their hearts singing, "I was glad when they said to me, 'Let us go to the house of the LORD!'" (Ps. 122:1)? How many followers of Jesus admonish one another, as C. S. Lewis explained to Sheldon Vanauken: "It is a Christian duty, as you know, for everyone to be as happy as he can."[3]

The example of Ignazio Silone stands as an unwitting summary of the findings of historians and sociologists about why the "lost generation" of baby boomers left "church culture" in droves of millions during the 1970s and '80s: When Silone was a teenager, he and his friends stopped going to Mass, not because they rejected the Christianity, but because the people who went began to bore them, and they perceived that the major concerns of the church were irrelevant to their needs.[4] In an interview with theologian Mary Hatch, she agrees that the boomers did not so much reject religion as refuse the embrace of an unenthralling institutional church, which they saw as a collection of bores: "Most mainline churches bore their members . . . stifle their imagination and pacify their emotions."[5] No wonder many boomers love the Lord, but hate organized religion.

If eternal life offers nothing fun . . . If eternal life offers nothing funny . . . If eternal life offers nothing sensual . . . If eternal life offers nothing creative . . . Then nothing doing! too many are saying. This was on the gravestone of an unknown child in the Suffolk churchyard, but it could be on many other tombstones as well:

> Came in,
> Walked about,
> Didn't like it,
> Walked out.

There will be a great deal of self-denial and pain in a fulfilled and fulfilling life of faith. But the church has failed to make pointedly the point of the Christian life: "To glorify God and enjoy God forever."[6] As Augustine said so emphatically, God is the ultimate object of enjoyment. Pleasure is a path to God if by pleasure one means not physical urges but the pleasing of God and fulfillment of being.[7] In God's presence is fullness of joy, the psalmist insisted (16:11), and in God's right hand are *"pleasures* forevermore."

Jesus is asked why his disciples don't fast on Wednesday and Friday like the Pharisees (Matt. 9:14-17; Mark 2:18-22; Luke 5:33-39). It is a good question. Fasting was a common custom in Jesus' day. The Pharisees were regular fasters (often two days a week, in memory of Moses' ascent and descent of Sinai),[8] and the Essenes were rigorous fasters. Jesus was known to fast himself. When? When he was "led by the Spirit" to prepare for spiritual warfare.

Why fast? To reach the highest and deep-

> ## *If you fast, you will give rise to sin for yourselves.*
>
> Gospel of Thomas *14*[9]

est levels of communion with God. A weekly fast is a good prescription for the body, mind, and spirit. There are physical, mental, and spiritual benefits of engaging "in fastings often" (2 Cor. 11:27 NKJV; cf. 2 Cor. 6:1-5)—they cleanse the body of impurities, the mind thinks better on an empty stomach, and one's spirit enters a tunnel that takes it from *chronos* to *kairos*. In fact, a forty-day tunnel (something Jesus shared with Moses, Elijah, and Buddha) may be the threshold that takes humans from narrow spiritual consciousness to deep spirituality and primary wisdom. John Wesley believed a weekly familiarity with fasting emboldens our love of life and enhances our enjoyment of food. Wesley's General Rules recommended weekly fasts, and early Methodists fasted every Friday.[10]

Jesus answers the question with another question. Does one fast at a wedding celebration? There are times to fast, and times to party. When I am with my disciples, what need is there for fasting? Being in one another's presence vitiated their need to fast. Jesus gives his followers, as a lasting memorial of his presence, not a fast but a feast, something Tertullian forgot when he argued in 210 A.D. that fasting was a better aid to faith than feasting.[11]

Jesus says his disciples would fast when the time was right. When Jesus leaves, then they will need to enlarge their consciousness and fast. But even when we follow Jesus into the wilderness, fasting and praying, Jesus issues warnings. There are benefits to fasting, and some things are accomplished only by "prayer and fasting."[12]

But be careful: "when you fast, do not be like the hypocrites, with a sad countenance. For they disfigure their faces that they may appear to men to be fasting. . . . When you fast, anoint your head and wash your face, so that you do not appear to men to be fasting" (Matt. 6:16-18 NKJV). It was as hard in Jesus' day as it is in our own to distinguish who is one of the "little guys," and who is just another "small man." One of the ways Jesus made the distinction was whether these three things were done in private: prayer, fasting, and giving.

The point of the Christian life is not to deny oneself and abnegate the self. Although a theology of sacrifice and service is a high priority in every walk with Jesus, one "loses oneself" and sacrifices not to "lose oneself" but toward the end of "finding oneself"—of gaining one's soul and pleasing God. John Piper in *Desiring God* argues that we are to fall in love with what God falls in love with, and then live like a hedonist.[13] Or in Augustine's best known, but least understood, statement, "Love God, and do what you will."

Besides, when fun is seen as "sinful," then "sin" becomes fun. Boredom, doldrums, defiant drabdom, and sickness are stones that the world has hung around the church's neck for too long. It's time to rip them off. Living is, or should be, lively. It's time the church declared war on dullness and sickness.

> *The dieter says: Sweets are bad; I cannot have them ever. The faster says: Sweets are good; I will not take them now. The dieter is condemned to bitter bondage, to a life which dares not let food in. But the faster is . . . preparing for a feast. His Lent leads to an Easter, and to mirth and weight of Glory.*
>
> *Robert Farrar Capon*[14]

When Jesus says to his disciples in frustration "How dull you are!" he spoke a prophetic as well as caustic word. H. L. Mencken enjoyed twitting Christians with "the chief contribution of Protestantism to human thought is its massive proof that God is a bore."[15] Political humorist Mark Russell said of Walter Mondale, son of a minister and married to the daughter of a minister: "Walter Mondale's charisma falls somewhere between a Presbyterian minister and a tree." Winston Churchill used to say "Broadly speaking, human beings may be divided into three classes: those who are billed to death, those who are worried to death and those who are bored to death."[16]

Why is "boredom" our most widespread ecclesiastical disease? The boredom of believing is an acute form of sickness (the relationship between boredom and disease is well documented[17]) whose primary symptom is the worship of a God people neither fear nor love. To be sure, there are some whose literary and historical judgments make boredom the opposite of bedlam. The great British historian A. J. P. Taylor, whose scholarship was virtually tone deaf to religion, bragged "I don't find Jesus a very interesting character, though he was obviously a good man."[18] Some people only find evil and hatred interesting. Some would only be happy if they saw the Body of Christ bubbling with bubbly.

It is possible to be both good and interesting, even good and exciting, even good and healthy. In fact, in the words of the early Latin Christian proverb, *Vivens homo gloria Dei* or "The glory of God is a person fully alive" or "The glory of God is a person fully in his or her life." The postmodern church must help people live so fully in the life God has given them that they can testify, "I'm having the time of my life being a follower of Jesus Christ." There is no more exciting, adventurous way to go through life than as a disciple of Jesus.

And here is part of our problem. If our mission statement to live a whole, healthy life requires us to know Christ and to make Christ known, what kind of Christ is being known? We are offering the world more a church-Jesus than a street-Jesus, more a program Jesus than a people Jesus. The widening gap between religion and spirituality is making our church-Jesus all the more problematic.

John Hyde was a missionary to India at the turn of the century. "Praying Hyde," as he was known, lived a life of prayer and sobriety. One day a non-Christian thought to make sport of John Hyde's seriousness. "Don't you think, Mr. Hyde, that a lady who dances can go to heaven?" He looked at her, and a huge smile broke out across his face. "I do not see how a lady can go to heaven *unless* she dances," he replied.[19] A dancer's adage goes something like this: "You will never become fully human until you dance."

II

It has not been pointed out often enough: There is a "revel" in revelation. Jesus loves a good party, and starts parties wherever he goes. Jesus takes the world both earnestly and festively. It is more than a little much to portray Jesus as a "first-century party animal," as some have done.[20] Jesus goes to parties with a purpose, parties that have a point, parties that glorify God and celebrate life and all its transitions in the spirit of God.

But Jesus' fun-seeking, party-loving side has too often been suppressed. Jesus looks for excuses to have a party, and seems to go to every good party he can. He especially enjoys festivals and Jewish family weddings, which abound in food, laughter, music, and dancing. In fact, one scholar has argued that "in all the Gospels there is never a hint that Christ was guilty of heterodoxy in his observance of feasts."[21] Jesus is present in Jerusalem for the official observance of Passover (John 2:13), Tabernacles (John 2:7), and Dedication (John 10:22). Charles Dickens was more right than he knew when he made a party, which occurs in *A Christmas Carol* every few pages, the purest expression of the Christmas spirit.

Jesus throws one party for five thousand people, and runs out of food. There is evidence of him bringing wine to parties, and some accuse him of drinking too much at these parties. How ironic, in the words of David Lowes Watson, that "inebriated behavior was the first Christian credential."[22] If Jesus had spoken fluent Latin, he would have been less likely to say with Descartes *Cogito ergo sum* ("I am because I think") than to say *Convivo ergo sum* ("I am because I party").

In her look at "the jubilant side of Jesus," theologian Elizabeth Barnes argues that at the wedding feast in Cana of Galilee "Jesus danced and cavorted and laughed, wine cup in hand, putting aside for a time the demands of his important ministry and the hard work he would resume on the morrow."[23]

Explicating "the paradox of self-sacrificial self-expression," Barnes shows how Jesus lived life "vigorously, richly, committedly, unreservedly, stumbling and rising, in other words, sacrificially. Only so does one travel the road modeled by Jesus the Christ."[24]

Asked to name her favorite Bible story, a six-year-old Sunday school student said it is the story of Jesus changing water into wine at the marriage feast in Cana. "What did you learn from the story?" the teacher inquires. The child answers: "When you have a wedding, it's a good idea to have Jesus at your party."

If "the poor" are those we consider worthy of receiving our charity, as Georg Simmel contends, Jesus reaches out beyond "the poor" to "the despised." Jesus throws parties for those not yet deemed "worthy" by the world of having parties thrown for them. He upsets the social applecart by associating with those society consider unclean. He even treats women as equals, and counts women among his best friends and followers. In the words of John Dominic Crossan, Jesus proclaims a kingdom of "Nuisances and Nobodies."[25]

Jesus does not say: "Come unto me, all you good people who are perfect and successful and I will lift you up." Jesus says: "Come unto me, all you who are weary and heavy laden and I will give you a good time." The recently discovered *Dialogue of the Savior* (65-66) includes this question from Matthew: "When will we find rest?" The Lord answered: "When you lay your burdens down!"[26] He even invites himself to dinner with despised tax collectors like Zacchaeus. Jesus has this very annoying habit of getting into bad company very quickly. He appears with "bad company" in public; he eats his meals with "bad company." Look at Jesus' party companions: adulterers, swindlers, prostitutes, peddlers, tax collectors, donkey-drivers, shepherds, tanners, and others.

When was the last time you ate dinner (at least knowingly) with these kinds of shady characters? Doing the right thing for the wrong reason is not Jesus' idea of being a saint. People who simply keep the rules are not necessarily God's people. The devil keeps the letter of the law. Jesus wants a right spirit within us.

Jesus lived out of the tradition that taught that mortals "look on the outward appearance, but the LORD looks on the heart" (1 Sam. 16:7). These words may mean more than we ever imagined if we place them within the context of the two hints given us about the physical appearance of Jesus: He looked older than he was (John 8:56-57) and he was ordinary-looking, with nothing striking about his features (Isa. 53:2 NKJV—"He has no form or comeliness; and when we see Him, there is no beauty that we should desire Him").

Like Charlie Halvey's pub in Michael Curtin's novel *The Plastic Tomato Cutter* (1993),[27] where a sign reads "The management reserves the right to serve everybody," Jesus reserved the right to party with everybody. Jesus partied with commoners—the Gentiles, sinners, the hoi polloi. Jesus enjoyed sitting with them, laughing, hearing their stories, and telling his own.

Few things got Jesus in more trouble than this. Jesus is never voted "One of the Outstanding Young Men

> **The sinner is at the heart of Christianity. No-one is as competent in the matter of Christianity as the sinner.**
>
> **No-one, unless it is the saint.**
>
> *Charles Péguy* [28]

in Nazareth" for precisely this reason. In kindergarten, kids are graded on how well they play with others. Jesus played and partied with everyone, the "down and out" as well as the "up and in": lepers, prostitutes, priests, scribes, centurions, crowds, children, disciples, Samaritans, Jews, Gentiles, slaves, free, politicians.

In a day when the religious establishment (and even the Qumran community) excluded outcasts, outlaws, the disabled, those with bodily defects, and those whose morality did not measure up, from tabling with "the righteous," these were the very ones Jesus invited to join him at table. Jesus felt comfortable around people with flaws, and set tables for them. In a day when the righteous prayed "Lord, send us the best people" Jesus prayed "Father, send us the people no one else wants."

In a day when gathering and reclining around a table necessitated taking off one's weapons and therefore becoming vulnerable to those at table with you ("You prepare a table before me in the presence of my enemies" [Ps. 23:5]), Jesus puts himself in a receiving posture and demonstrates a theology of receiving before a theology of giving.

In a day when one reclined on cushions while eating the Passover meal to symbolize the rest God gave to Israel through God's covenant faithfulness in the exodus from Egypt and entrance into the Promised Land, Jesus "rests" with outsiders and the outcast.

In a day when sharing a meal meant entering a relationship, Jesus shares mealtime experiences that cut across all boundaries that divide, and rearranged all categories of class, race, type, and gender. Jesus knows no such thing as a "party of one."

In a day when no man was supposed to speak to a woman in public, Jesus parties with women—even women who supposedly "defiled" him by their caress and conversation. We fail to see how unusual it is simply to have the stories in the biblical record of the widow of Nain, Simon's mother-in-law, the Canaanite woman, and the woman who was hemorrhaging. Jesus' ministry of touch reached to even the "untouchables." In fact, Jesus never met an "untouchable."

Especially the hemorrhaging woman. Women during their menstrual periods are ceremonially "unclean" according to Levitical law. They cannot be even touched by a righteous man. The woman who reaches out and grabs the "hem of his garment" actually touched one of the 613 tassels hanging from Jesus' prayer shawl, or *tallit,* which Jesus wore whenever he went outside. Every shawl is embroidered with 613 tassels around the fringe—one tassel for each of the laws of the Torah. The point of these tassels is not to show off one's knowledge of the Torah (see Jesus' criticism of long tassels in Matthew 25). The purpose of these tassels is to symbolize that when one prays, one literally wraps oneself in the healing, life-giving Word of God. That is why when the woman who has been "unclean" for twelve years touches one of Jesus' tassels, Jesus does not recoil in horror but reaches down, holds, heals, and helps her to her feet.

> *There is nothing wrong with going after what we want in life. The hard part is enjoying it once we get it.*
>
> Daisy Brown

Jesus even enters into a serious theological discussion about God with a woman. But to make bad matters worse (women were not considered "worthy" enough to hold any kind of serious discussion, especially one about God), Jesus engages in this profound spiritual conversation with a profligate woman (she has had *five* husbands). Here is a notorious sinner; and here is Jesus, the "friend of sinners," affirming her and taking her thoughts and feelings seriously. Jesus is so close to Mary Magdalene, and she figures so prominently in the resurrection story, that one scholar calls her the "apostle to apostles."[29]

Jesus spends his ministry walking among sinners and partying with sinners. Paul reminded the church at Rome, "While we were *yet* sinners, Christ died for us" (Rom. 5:8 NASB). That is why the world doesn't need more "church suppers." The world needs more dinner parties. A youthful Mao liked to say that "a revolution is not a dinner party." For Jesus a revolution is a dinner party.

No wonder the Lord's Table has been called "the longest table in the world"—over twenty-five thousand miles of fellowship. As symbolized in the "table talk" of his fellowship meals, Jesus preaches a message for "nobodies" that made those of notoriety sit up and take notice. These "nobodies" are not just non-Pharisees. As E. P. Sanders has argued, "sinners" here means not just the ritually impure but "the wicked . . . those who sinned wilfully and heinously and who did not repent."[30]

Jesus does not say, "Get your affairs straightened out, and then I'll eat with you." Jesus does not say, "You want to come to my table? Then shape up." Jesus eats with people in the midst of their brokenness, people that good people then as today do not find acceptable. Jesus identifies with people precisely where they are hurting most and fearing most and failing most. Jesus eats with the good, the bad, and the both. Jesus violates Jewish law by extending too much mercy on sinners.

In Jesus' day, illness meant exposure to immediate economic distress for a person without resources. One scholar writes that "The economic threat of disease . . . to the lower and middle class was grave, graver perhaps than at any later time."[31] Illness meant inability to work.

This is illustrated by an apocryphal version of the story of the healing of the man with a withered hand (from Matt. 12:9-14). In the apocryphal version, the sick man is identified as a stonemason. He makes his request of Jesus: "I was a mason and earned my livelihood with my hands; I beseech thee, Jesus, to restore to me my health that I may not with ignominy have to beg for my bread."[32] Illness here is not just a physical problem, but a social and economic problem.

These subtle linkages of socioeconomic status and health both compound and confound the "healthcare crisis" in our day as well as in Jesus' own. The poor are still being deprived of resources for medical healing. In fact, the medicalization of so many social ills (from drug abuse to kleptomania to compulsive gambling to spousal abuse) obscures the fact that maybe we ought to look at some illnesses as having a socioeconomic rootage, and not just at some social ills as having a health basis.

Healthcare must be decommodified: It is not a commodity but a right. The commodification of healthcare has given us an economy where healthcare costs now make up 13 percent of the gross national product (GNP), and will account for 17 percent of the GNP by the year 2000. In fact, the Southern Baptist Convention alone spent $64 million in medical benefits for pastors in 1990, with the number one and number two claims for payments being for maternity and stress-related illnesses.

> *After a good dinner, one can forgive anybody, even one's relatives.*
>
> Oscar Wilde

Jesus is the enemy of exclusivity. I am reminded of this by a Jewish couple who are major donors to United Theological Seminary. When I asked them over lunch one day what country club they were members of, they were aghast. Didn't I know them any better than that, they demanded? "All country clubs are based on one principle, and one principle only, Len. That is exclusion. Why would anyone want to join something where the only reason for its existence is exclusionary—to exclude your sisters and brothers?"

The "scandal" of a love that announced "more joy in heaven over one sinner who repents . . . " (Luke 15:7) wrecks Jesus' career and brings him to an early grave. In fact, it is Jesus' adamant mission to the poor of society (Matt. 7:12; Mark 9:35; Luke 10:29-37), as much as his strident denunciations of establishment powers, that probably tip him off to the likelihood of a violent death.

III

There is a *Peanuts* cartoon in which Charles Schulz has Lucy telling her brother Linus to get with it, get on the ball, get involved. As Linus stands sucking his thumb and hanging on for dear life to his security blanket, Lucy says:

> You can't drift along forever. You have to direct your thinking. You have to decide whether you're going to be a liberal or a conservative. You have to take some sort of stand. You have to associate yourself with some sort of cause.
>
> Whereupon Linus pulls his thumb out of his mouth, puts down his security blanket, and asks Lucy: "Are there any openings on the lunatic fringe?"

Jesus is looked upon as a member of the "lunatic fringe" of his day—both his enemies and his friends think of him in this way. There has been much debate about why Jesus is "Yeshua ben Miryam" or "son of Mary" and not "Yeshua ben Joseph" as he should have been called. Stephen Mitchell argues that Jesus is literally in the categories of his day "a bastard." At least he is derided for being a child conceived out of wedlock: "You son of Mary" (Mark 6:3; cf. John 8:41) is the first century equivalent of "You son of a bitch." Whatever his status, he is perceived as a bastard by his peers, and maligned accordingly. No wonder we have these words of Luke 6:26 (REB): "Alas for you when all speak well of you." The taunts and mockeries over his "illegitimacy" help shape Jesus' attitudes toward the poor and outcasts of society.[33]

> *He was a stranger to the feasts of life.*
>
> James Joyce, on the spiritually alienated human

But on that lunatic fringe, Jesus is able to say to people who never heard these words before: "You did not choose me but I chose you" (John 15:16). Jesus' whole life is a pattern of choosing. Jesus is a "choosing" Savior who testifies to a God who chooses: "I choose," Jesus said God says (Matt. 20:14 NJB).

There are many faith choices out there—"God doesn't exist," "God doesn't care," "God doesn't care about me," and so on. People of Jesus' day are going along in their miserable lives when one day they hear Jesus "choose" them—and that choice makes all the difference in their lives.

That choice makes all the difference in my life. (Some people sow wild oats. I planted a prairie.) That same choice makes all the difference in our lives. This does not mean we become some kind of "chosen" people. This does mean that, like our Savior, we too become a "choosing" people with special regard for those the world never chooses—the left-outs, the losers, the lost, the lunatics.

Each of us must make faith choices. Will we "choose" others as part of our faith choice that they might "choose" the God who loves the world so much that Jesus was sent to show us just how much?

* * *

CHAPTER EIGHT

Come Apart So You Don't Come Apart

* * *

When the world gets too much for Jesus, when things simply get too hectic ("What stress I am under," Jesus exclaimed in Luke 12:50), Jesus takes off. How does Jesus deal with stress—with the stress of rejection, of despair, of misunderstanding? He changes focus. Rather than *take out* his stress on others, Jesus *takes off,* and lets nature revive his flagging spirit.

Sigmund Freud was more than the founder of psychoanalysis. He was the first patient of psychoanalysis, and the first person to be cured of a serious mental illness by psychoanalysis.[1] In other words, Freudian analysis allegedly self-cured Freud. Unlike Freud and psychotherapy, which instructed humans to solve their problems by looking within and turning inward, Jesus believes that our physical and mental well-being often requires a switch in atmosphere, a change of pace and place.[2] "Going within" doesn't solve our problems; self-absorption usually causes more problems than it cures.

Jesus gets people outside themselves. He doesn't show people how to get within themselves so much as he devises ways to get people outside themselves. James Hillman is not the first to advocate a psychological approach that turns away

> ## Blessed are the solitary . . . for you will find the Kingdom.
>
> *A new beatitude from the* Gospel of Thomas 49[3]

from an inward focus and reorients us to the *anima mundi* and the condition of the world. It is Jesus who taught life's paradox that we go *within* ourselves by getting *outside* ourselves. Intimacy with oneself is found through involvement in the world.

For Jesus, soulcraft is worldcraft. Jesus goes outward *from* the self, and engages with what was all around him, before he goes inward *to* the self. Jesus is psychologically strong and physically healthy because his life is patterned around alternating periods of society and solitude, intensity, and insularity. For Jesus, a healthy soul means a person not introspecting on a couch but a person climbing a mountain, boating in the water, or goatwalking in the desert. When my mountain ancestors dismissed one another with "Go jump in the lake," they were prescribing something more profound than they knew. They were outlining a strategy for healthy living.

Sometimes Jesus "came apart" by himself where no one could find him (Matt. 14:23). He withdrew from being the center of attention ("everyone is looking for you") to find his true center through prayer "retreats." Jesus disengaged from people so that he might engage more fully with life. Jesus worked through some of life's most negative emotions (anger, sadness, fear, loneliness) through deep silence more than through "talking it out." Indeed, Jesus' silence seems to deepen toward the end.[4]

Sometimes he "came apart" and sought solace in the solitude

of a garden olive grove. He gets up early and escapes to the gardens to meditate and pray (Mark 1:35). Jesus used the garden as a place of prayer—well-being has always been found in a garden—and his first post-resurrection appearance as the Second Adam took place as a gardener. When Jesus was close to mental and physical breakdown (repeated falling on the ground [Mark 14:35; Luke 22:44] and the rare phenomenon of hematidrosis or sweating blood are symptoms of severe mental anguish), the disciples gathered around him in the Garden of Gethsemane and tried to become for him a healing community (see also Matt. 26:38; Mark 14:34).

> *In solitude our intimacy with each other is deepened.*
>
> Henri Nouwen

Sometimes Jesus withdrew to the mountains (Mark 3:13). He often headed for the hills where he found help from El Shaddai (God of Mountains). One time he became a mountain climber and "led them up a high mountain" (Matt. 17:1).

Other times Jesus withdraws to the lake (Mark 3:7) and identifies with the water. His baptism at the River Jordan took place most likely without any bystanders: "After all the people had been baptized, Jesus also was baptized . . . " (Luke 3:21 GNB). The crowds had come to the river and gone before Jesus arrived, probably leaving John the Baptist and Jesus alone.

Other times Jesus wants to be with people. He asked his disciples, "Come away with me." "Come away to a deserted place all by yourselves and rest a while" (Mark 6:31).

> *Get yourself up on a high mountain.*
>
> (Isa. 40:9 NASB)

How does one "find oneself"? Jesus teaches that we find ourselves by losing ourselves in the "other." The "other" can be people, or it can be places. Jesus' favorite people to get lost in, as we have seen, were the broken and the abandoned. Jesus' favorite places to get lost in were the desert, the mountains, and the seashore.

> *The miracle is not to walk on water. The miracle is to walk on the green Earth in the present moment, to appreciate the peace and beauty that is available now.*
>
> *Thich Nhat Hanh* [5]

Some scholars have even divided Mark's Gospel according to the "retreats" (better known as advances?) of Jesus. The desert taught Jesus about courage, solitude, limits, and inner strength. The mountains taught Jesus about dreams, exhilaration, and aspiration. The water taught Jesus about cooperation, softness, trust, control, and the relationship between content and container.

Jesus knows when to slow down and when to stop completely and withdraw. He is a student of the psalmist, who summoned everything that lives and that breathes—sun, moon, stars, birds, and sea creatures—to praise the Lord (adapted from Ps. 150:6 and Psalm 148). He was a student of Job:

> Now ask the beasts,
> and they will teach you;

> And the birds of the air,
>   and they will tell you;
> Or speak to the earth,
>   and it will teach you;
> And the fish of the sea
>   will explain to you. (12:7-8 NKJV)

He admonishes his disciples to come to their sacramental senses: "Consider the lilies" (Luke 12:27) and "Consider the ravens" (Luke 12:24). In the humblest of creatures there awaits the grandest of discoveries.

I

Want to reach the beyond? Enter your world. Want to understand the nature of scripture? Understand the scripture of nature.[6] Want to pack more punch into your life? "Consider the lilies," Jesus says.

"Consider the lilies" is not the equivalent of "Stop and smell the roses." We love to tell people "Stop and smell the roses" because it doesn't threaten us or change us. Once we've stopped for a few minutes or even a few days to smell the roses (that's what in the business world is called a "vacation," or in the academic world "the leisure of the theoried class," also known as sabbatical), we go right on with our lives as if nothing had happened, leaving the roses behind.

Psychologist Howard Glazer calls the kinds of stop-and-smell-the-roses vacations we take "behavioral Rorschach tests." He identifies five vacation styles among Manhattan's movers and shakers.[7] First are the "Power Players" who don't mask their taking the office with them on vacation. They're on the beach with their virtual office, or hiking the mountain with their cellular phones hooked to their ears. They basically transfer their work to a different location.

Next there are the "Stress Fighters." These movers and shakers vacation by making up in a couple of weeks what they should have been doing all year. They diet, they exercise, they eat right, they sleep. "They're on a mission, not a vacation."

Many of them are now "wildering," and you can tell a "Stress Fighting" vacationer by the ubiquitous mineral water bottle.

The third category of vacationers is the "Schedulers," who most often go on tours where every minute can be filled with stimulation so there is no downtime, no unstructured time, no spontaneous time, no facing of what "Schedulers" left behind. This is a popular care for the carers.

Fourth, there are the "Fun Worshipers." This group most resembles the power players, except they totally avoid the office. No mail. No work addiction. This group is going to have the greatest return on fun in the shortest investment of time.

Last, the "Fugitives" fell exhaustedly from their jobs into heavy vacation rituals of partying, long days' journeys into nights, and so forth. Some of these "Fugitives" take vacations through illnesses, for they have worked so hard and ground themselves down so far. Baby boomers comprise a hefty portion of fugitives.

All of these five vacation styles are really subcategories of one not mentioned: "Cheaters." "Cheaters" are "Power Players," "Stress Fighters," "Fun Worshipers," "Schedulers," and "Fugitives" who say they are taking a vacation, who genuinely believe they are stopping to smell the roses, but who really only stop long enough to say they stopped.

Jesus gives us a "Consider-the-lilies" vacation style that is best described as "advances" rather than "retreats." There is a healing, quickening power to "advances" that we have only begun to discover, but their potential for healing is maximized when they become a ritual part of one's everyday life (even to the point of taking minute-long vacations) and they are diverse in style.

Nike founder Phil Knight is so convinced that the best ideas come from the "strangeness" of the beach, the "otherness" of nature, and not the "familiarity" of the office that he built a corporate office complex that is more like a campus with ponds, jogging trails, tennis courts, weight rooms, and basketball courts. Claude Rosenberg, founder of Rosenberg Capital Management, has two quiet rooms set up in the office for people to come apart, and he requires vacations of all his employees so that they might tune in to other realities besides themselves.

The answer is not in any "retreat"—though I contend that leaders and their spouses need at least three prayer advances a year where they reset dreams in their relationship, renegotiate time commitments, discuss finances, and define outcomes. The answer is back where you came from. But when the way looks drear, and the path not clear, it behooves us to take the advice of the risen Christ to his dejected disciples: "Return to Galilee." Go back to those days you spent with God on the mountaintops. Return to your joy. Rekindle the fire. Nurture your first love—and you will find the divine quickening in your soul once more.

The word "quickening" is an old word that names the first sensation of new life forming in the womb and the movement of that new life within the mother. But as Jean Shinoda Bolen points out, that word is also derived from the tradition of pilgrims, "who go to sacred places to 'quicken' the divinity within themselves, to experience spiritual awakening or receive a blessing or become healed. The seeker embarks on a journey with a receptive soul and hopes to find divinity there."[8] Advances can "quicken" a sense of the sacred as one is awakened to the God who is, in Paul's formula, "over all and through all and in all" (Eph. 4:6 NASB).

Jesus did not say "Stop and smell the lilies." Jesus said "Consider the lilies." "Consider" is not a lazy, leisurely word. It does not mean the "pleasing contemplation of the beautiful" as one commentator put it. It does not mean to give something your "passing note" or "passing nod" or "passing fancy." It means to give something everything you've got. In the modern world we were too busy gilding the lilies (and ourselves) to notice them, much less consider them. I saw this card recently showing two cows with the caption: "As you travel along the road of life, be sure to stop awhile and eat the flowers."

Philo used this word "consider" to describe the attempt of our being to perceive God. "Consider" has everything to do with the process of knowing God, which is as close a definition to spirituality as the Bible gives. This is the verb in Luke 12:24, 27; this is the word in Hebrews 3:1. When Jesus says "consider them," he means to give "them" careful examination and constant application. He means to learn thoroughly, to let the presence of this truth sink into your deepest being; he means to let this beauty reawaken faith and obedience and worship in your soul.

Jesus' flower-power faith communed with nature. In this way he drew strength. He never lost his capacity to appreciate natural beauty or the way, in the poetic words I heard somewhere, "all that came to be was alive with his life." Indeed, he was never out of touch with the beauty around him. In spending time in the mountains, on the seashore, or in the desert, he demonstrated how the very air we breathe is alive with meaning. "Wild air, world-mothering air" Hopkins called it in his remarkable poem "The Blessed Virgin Compared to the Air We Breathe." This is God's world. God is alive in it, and God is bonded to it.

II

Jesus was far from "the most out-of-doors man that ever lived" as one bishop tried to style him.[9] But he did find every opportunity to insert the natural in the holy, and the holy in the natural. Jesus never felt the need to prettify nature. He accepted creation on its own terms, and used nature so extensively as teaching tools that he is accurately called a "nature theologian." Most of Jesus' parables assume a relationship between the natural and the spiritual world. Jesus believed that there was not mere analogy but an inward affinity between the processes that are at work in the natural world and those that govern the world of the spirit.

Compare Jesus' use of images, most of which were drawn from the out-of-doors, with the kind of writing one finds in the rest of the Second Testament, especially Paul. Wendell Berry argues that "I don't think it is enough appreciated how much an outdoor book the Bible is. It is a 'hypaethral book,' such as Thoreau talked about—a book open to the sky. It is best read and understood outdoors, and the farther outdoors the better. Or that has been my experience of it. Passages that within walls seem improbable or incredible, outdoors seem merely natural. This is because outdoors we are confronted everywhere with wonders; we see that the miraculous is not extraordinary but the common mode of existence. It is our daily bread."[10]

Jesus was not just close to the natural world. Jesus did not seem to distinguish between himself and nature. He saw himself as part of nature, in the midst of creation, not separate from nature. Jesus exhibited what the Native American peoples have called the "long body"—a larger self that embraces other people, places, animals, and planet Earth itself.[11] He didn't see himself as an agrarian, to be sure, but notice how often Jesus "seems to stand *outside* cities," theologian Geoffrey Lilburne observes.

"Jesus, then, lives his life 'in place.' Not for him the placelessness of our modern experience. He is at home in the environment and can reflect deeply the presence and the resonance of the environment in his parables and aphorisms, in his dialogues and stories."[12]

Jesus once warned his disciples that if humans fail to praise, the very rocks will cry out. He was making more than a rhetorical point. This is exactly what happened. When he was on the cross, everyone ran and hid. No one stayed to praise him or stand by him (except some women whose testimony couldn't count and John), not even his closest friends the disciples, "who should themselves have been at the foot of the cross, if not hanging on other crosses round about."[13] But when everyone else was silent, or using their lips to give Jesus the kiss of betrayal (Judas) or the kiss-off of denial (Peter), the rocks cried out.

While Jesus hangs on the cross, the earth is shaken (Matthew uses the word *seio* here, from which our word seismograph is partially derived), the rocks (*petrai,* the crust of the earth) are split (Matt. 27:51*b*—the word used here is *schizo*) and the Temple curtain is rent in twain. Just as the heavens were "opened" (literally "awakened" or "torn apart") at Jesus baptism (Mark 1:10), so the earth itself is awakened and torn apart at his crucifixion. The whole earth continues its "groaning in travail awaiting the day of its redemption."

I reread the Gospels with an eye to Jesus' interaction with the animal kingdom, and am struck by the ways in which the Gospels portray an animal-friendly lifestyle. Jesus is born in a stable "manger" (or if not here, on the ground floor of a two-level Bethlehem house, in a room where animals were led in at night). At his baptism a descending dove appears to bring a Noahlike sign of God's good pleasure, and Jesus himself likens the Spirit to a dove.[14] In the desert, after being tempted by the enemies of heaven and earth, he is with

COPENHAGEN

Here lies

Copenhagen

The charger ridden by

The duke of Wellington

The entire day, at the

Battle of Waterloo

Born 1808 Died 1836

God's Humbler Instrument,

Though Meaner Clay

Should Share the Glory

of That Glorious Day.

Epitaph on the chestnut stallion's grave at the Ice House Paddock at Stratfield Saye House the wild animals and is ministered to by angels (Mark 1:13). In a world of wolves, Jesus says to "be wise as serpents and harmless as doves" (Matt. 10:16 NKJV). Just as Jonah discovered under a gourd God's concern for the cows of Nineveh (Jonah 4), so Jesus' disciples were taught God's love for the sparrows of Jerusalem (Matt. 10:29).

Carl Jung was not the first to sense that only the animals are truly pious, for only the animals willy-nilly do the will of God (the animals live exactly as God intends them to live; only human beings deviate from God's will).[15] Jesus celebrated the birds of the air, who toil not nor are anxious about the morrow. When Jesus and his disciples neared Bethphage, he sent them ahead to fetch a donkey (*onos*), which was attached to her colt. Not wanting to separate the mother from her colt, Jesus had them both brought to him, and ended up riding the as yet unridden colt in his unglamourous, even ungainly messianic entrance into Jerusalem (Matt. 21:2, 7). One of the most common texts on gravestones is "the Lord hath need of him" (Mark 11:3 KJV), words originally spoken about an ass.[16]

There is no record that Jesus ever offers animal sacrifices, or encourages his disciples to do so. In fact, the commercial corruption in the Temple that triggered the whipcracking side of Jesus' personality may have included abuses in the custom of animal sacrifices. His compassion for the outcast and oppressed overflows into anger at the trade in sacrificial animals in the great courtyard of the Temple, the religious, social, and commercial center of the city.

The anger of Jesus is not the subject of very many sermons. The prophet Nehemiah got so angry one time that he. . . . Well, let Nehemiah tell what he did himself: "I contended with them and cursed them and beat some of them and pulled out their hair" (Neh. 13:25). Now, *that's* angry. But Jesus had his confrontational moments as well: "You brood of vipers!" he said to one group of people.[17] "Go tell that fox . . . " Jesus says of Herod (Luke 13:32).

When Jesus picks up a rope used to tether one of the animals and begins flailing it over his head, overturning the merchants' tables and thereby freeing the caged animals and birds, his "temple tantrum" may be directed at least in part against the wanton selling and slaughter of animals at huge profits for the high priests and their temple merchant cronies. A house of prayer and peace has been turned into a den of thievery and violence. Jesus didn't just clear the moneychangers out of the temple, Gore Vidal writes in *Live from Golgotha*, "he lowered the prime rate."[18] Or in the words of another biblical scholar, "What Jesus did was like attacking the Bank of America."

Little wonder animal sacrifice has not been a part of the Christian tradition from Jesus' day onward. Christians were some of the most outspoken enemies of the amphitheater games, which featured gladiators in the late afternoon, public executions of criminals at midday, and gory beast hunts in the morning. Jesus' life does not argue for a rights-based moral theory of "animal liberation" that one finds in the writings of Peter Singer and Tom Regan. But his life taken in its entirety is an argument that we need to see ourselves in a different posture than we have vis-à-vis animals.[19] Descartes said animals had no souls and were in the same category as machines. Thomas Aquinas said animals could be cursed as "satellites of Satan." Jesus saw things very differently.

My Anglo-Saxon ancestors settled the Appalachian Mountains, where many started out as Baptists and Methodists but ended up in the Holiness and Pentecostal movements. West Virginia snakehandlers never kill the snake. No matter how many people the snake might bite, or even kill, the snakes are treated lovingly, respectfully. These people seek to live in harmony with nature, not to destroy it, even its deadliest serpents.[20]

Ever wonder why so many medical waiting rooms have an aquarium? Companion pets exercise beneficial effects on human health. Alick Hartley's *The Tale of Three Dogs* (1993) is a gem of a book. It describes how one widower whose world was restricted by illness was brought back to new life and new depths of faith in God through the simple presence of a dog in his life. One epidemiologic study after another has shown that having pets can lower blood pressure and heart rate as well as reduce mental distress. Those who share their lives with pets have higher morale and lower rates of depression. They also tend to get more regular exercise (for obvious reasons).

Alan Beck, who heads the Center for Applied Ethology and Human-Animal Interaction at the Purdue University School of Veterinary Medicine, argues that pets fill the role of an infant or young child in a household.[21] An Australian study reported in 1992 documents a correlation between pet ownership and reduction in cardiovascular risk.

But the most extensive investigation of companion animals was done by epidemiologist Judith Siegel of UCLA. She found that 37 percent of participants who owned pets made fewer visits to the doctor than those without animal companions. She also discovered that pets functioned as a "stress buffer" for those suffering grief and loss, as well as a curative force for those recovering from acute illness.[22] Of 92 people admitted to a coronary care unit, those with pets were more likely to be alive one year later than those without animals. No wonder there is a medical movement toward "prescription pets," and an organization (The Delta Society) devoted to pulling together information about the health benefits of companion animals.[23]

Jesus comes apart by embracing nature, and protecting animals.

III

When God became incarnate in Jesus of Nazareth, God did not just enter human history. God entered the creation story. God entered the history of this planet as well as the history of people.

Jesus doesn't die for a cause such as the demise of the Roman Empire. Jesus dies for love—love for people, and love for creation ("For God so loved the cosmos . . . " reads the Greek of John 3:16). The redemption offered by Jesus the Christ is one that restores balance and harmony and beauty to creation. Or in the words of Ephesians, it is "the universe, everything in heaven and on earth," that is to "be brought into a unity in Christ" (1:10 REB). Just as nature suffered when the crown of God's creation chose to become its clown, so nature is to be redeemed as part of our salvation. Christ covers everything in the new birth.

When we come apart, particularly when we become a part of God's creation, we assume a responsibility to nurture and protect what God has put together. If we don't accept that responsibility, then we are in effect eliminating our purpose on earth.

The following dialogue took place in the comic strip *Calvin and Hobbes:*

CALVIN: I've been thinking Hobbes.
HOBBES: On a weekend?
CALVIN: Well, it wasn't on purpose. . . . I believe history is a force. . . . Its unalterable tide sweeps all people and institutions along its unrelenting path. Everything and everyone serves history's single purpose.
HOBBES: And what is that purpose?
CALVIN: Why, to produce ME, of course! I'm the end result of history!
HOBBES: You?
CALVIN: Think of it! Thousands of generations lived and died to produce my exact, specific parents, whose reason for being, obviously, was to produce ME.[24]

In his *Life on Earth* (1979), David Attenborough plots the history of life on Earth on the timescale of one year. If evolution started on 1 January, based on that scale humans "did not appear until the evening of 31 December."[25] Everything in the cosmos, which has a much longer history than humanity, was covered in Christ's redemptive suffering (Col. 1:20). The new community in Christ breaks down all barriers—cultural, sexual, economic, social, ecological (Gal. 3:27-28). *All* things are reconciled in him.

The salvation offered by Jesus the Christ, which establishes our reason for being, is ecocentric, not egocentric. When theologian Jürgen Moltmann passionately calls for a "cosmic interpretation of Christ's death and resurrection,"[26] he is challenging a Christian community whose horizons are wrongly limited to the human world (Rom. 8:19-23). The Greek expression is *pase te ktisei,* and the singular feminine of the noun *ktisis* means "creation," a comprehensive phrase for all created things, animate and inanimate. When Mark quotes Jesus as saying "Preach the gospel to all creation [*ktisis*]" (Mark 16:15 NASB), there is nothing to suggest that we ought to limit the proclamation to the human world.

Jesus lives out of an understanding that God's covenant with Noah was between God and the earth (Gen. 9:16). Jesus' ecological agapism even takes the form of a declaration and promise: "When I am lifted up from the earth, [I] will draw *all things* to myself."[27] Martin Luther's Preface to the Epistle to the Romans says that a faith that is "living, busy, active, powerful" will issue in a believer that is "joyful, bold, and *full of warm affection toward God and all created things."*

Christianity is an ecological religion. The 1960s took potshots at any number of easy targets, especially the Christian faith, and blamed it for the environmental degradation of planet Earth. The truth is just the opposite. "The Bible is so detailed in its description of attitudes which should inform care of the earth that it has been likened to a 'manufacturer's handbook.' With this 'handbook' for operators, we have the instructions for smooth operation—but we have to follow them."[28] Ecopsychologist Theodore Roszak calls our lack of ethics about our planetary home "the epidemic psychosis of our time." He adds: "A Culture that can do so much to damage the planetary fabric that sustains it, yet continues along its course unimpeded, is mad with the madness of a deadly compulsion."[29]

Jesus could read the "signs of the times" as well as the "signs of the skies." Homo sapiens, our native habitat the savannah, were designed to deal with short-term threats rather than long-term dangers.[30] We can react to the "signs of the skies," and are fleet of foot to escape marauding elephants, rampaging fires, bared-teeth tigers and whites-of-their-eyes warriors.

> # The whole landscape
> # a manuscript
> # We had lost the skill
> # to read.
>
> *John Montague*[32]

But Jesus calls us to read the distant early warning signals as well, to see the "signs of the times"[31] that have much longer fuses, to hear the cries from the future that beckon us to change before it's too late. Jesus was concerned about the end of the world. Long-term exposure to low-level radiation can be as deadly as high dosages. Similarly, long-term exposure to only slightly visible problems are as deadly as short-term exposure to the more visible problems. The apostle Paul, after contending that what can be known about God is partly revealed by the natural world, asserts that we remain oblivious to the truth because we "have bound the truth under a spell through injustice."[33]

Two of the loudest cries? The overpopulation and over-consumption of planet Earth, a home increasingly damaged by human parasitism. And waste. Amoebic organisms grow and grow until they literally die from their own waste. We are proving ourselves descendants of amoebas.

What Maria Cherkavosa, the head of the Socio-Ecological Union in Moscow, called the communists' "cannibalism of their country" applies to other nation-states as well. Jacques Cousteau tells of a flight of sparrows over Mexico City. The birds fell from the sky "like rain on rooftops and in the streets." Not one made it through the polluted air of the city.[34] Just as Jesus testified to a God who cares about sparrows falling out of their nests as well as hairs falling out of our heads, so the church must claim the environment as a theological, as well as health, issue. God-bondedness is creation-bondedness.

Similar nightmare scenarios can be sketched about wolves that are infertile (Michigan's Isle Royale National Park), elephants born without tusks (South Africa's Addo National Park), and lions with no immune systems (Tanzania's Ngonongoro Crater). In the Gulf of St. Lawrence, a dead beluga whale cannot be touched without gloves and face masks. It is classified as "toxic waste" on account of the concentration of toxins its body harbors.[35] The larger issue, however, is not just a single species, but an entire ecosystem. There are approximately five thousand fires now burning in the Amazon Basin, as the tropical rain forest ecosystem is in danger of extinction.

"Decreation" is the word used by essayist/naturist Bill McKibben to describe the human dismantling of the whole of creation, especially through two "decreations": first, climactic changes that affect every square inch of the Earth; second, the permanent loss of more than one hundred species of plants and animals per day.

Climactic "decreations" can be breathed. The amount of oxygen in the air is getting smaller and smaller. The amount of carbon dioxide is getting greater and greater. This leaves us literally panting for breath—Who knows but that the most prized drug of the twenty-first century may be acetazolamide, which fights the debilitating effects of oxygen starvation?

Species "decreations" can be seen . . . sometimes. Our bodies are hosts to millions of creatures invisible to us but active in and on our bodies, including forehead mites that live in hair follicles and sebaceous glands, wormlike creatures with spidery heads and monstrous bodies that, despite small biomass, reflect immense diversity.[36] Of the 20,000 native plants in the U.S., some 4,200 are threatened with extinction; 750 of these extinctions are imminent within the next decade. Planet Earth is losing a total of 100,000 species every year, the

> ## Nature is not out there. We are in it.
>
> *Sigmund Kvaløy,*
> *Eco-philosopher*[37]

majority of which (invertebrates) we've never seen or classified. What are the long-term chances of bass fish when they are being "hunted" with sonar fish finders once reserved for the nuclear submarine *Nautilus*?

Mountaineer and naturalist Jack Turner speaks about "the final loss"—the point we are fast approaching when environmental loss will no longer require our help, but will achieve a momentum all its own. When "the final loss" point is reached, we will have passed the point of no return. The degradation of the environment will happen willy-nilly.

One basis on which God will judge each one of us is this: How have you treated the earth? (Rev. 11:18). It is impossible to commune with Jesus within the natural world if you are perpetrating losses in nature. Rubbishing the creation while worshiping the Creator is sacrilege.[38] When in 1855 the English-born James Mason Hutchings took the first tourists to see the Calaveras Grove in California, they saw what came to be known as "God's

> **What would the world be,**
> **once bereft**
> **Of wet and of wildness?**
> **Let them be left,**
> **O let them be left, wildness**
> **and wet;**
> **Long live the weeds and**
> **the wilderness yet.**
>
> *Gerard Manley Hopkins*[39]

First Temples," mammoth trees that took five men three weeks to take down (two and a half days alone for toppling). Watching the loggers take down this half million feet of lumber, Hutchings wrote that what they were doing "was a sacrilegious act."[40] What they did with the trees once they were down was even more sacrilegious. One trunk of a tree they planed down and made into a two-lane bowling alley. Another sequoia was made into a dance floor for tourists, where at an Independence Day celebration thirty-two persons danced four sets of cotillion at one time, without anyone feeling crowded one bit.

Here is what is done to protect something beautiful that human hands have created—such as the Declaration of Independence those previously mentioned tourists were celebrating. We build a rotunda in the National Archives around it. We put it in a one-ton bombproof vault. We put it behind three inches of bulletproof glass, and station guards all around it. We don't let anyone look at it unless through green ultraviolet filters. We spend $3.3 million just to monitor its condition, and assess how best to preserve its fading ink.

What would we do if Michelangelo had painted a picture of a spotted owl? Here is what we would do—we would declare it one of the world's "priceless treasures" and do everything humanly possible to protect it and preserve it. We might even go to war over keeping it. What we wouldn't think of doing to it, even if we were planning on stealing it, would be to take a knife to it, much less a chainsaw.

But when God creates a spotted owl, when we're talking about a "Work of God" or a "Work of Nature" rather than a "Work of van Gogh" or a "Work of Michelangelo," we treat it with disregard and disdain. Are we scared of the wilderness without and the wild things of nature because we are scared of the wilderness within and the wild things of the Spirit?

In the spring of 1995, I was asked by the Presbyterians, Episcopalians, Southern Baptists, and United Methodists to come to the fastest growing spot of ground in North America—Naples, Florida—to lead a city-wide crusade. In a mid-December planning session with the four pastors involved, I stayed in the home of Tom and Martha Talton. They lived next to Molasses Swamp, a magical twenty-three acres of wildlife, wildflowers, wetlands, and native wilderness that I explored in a golf cart and on foot.

When I returned to Naples a few months later for the crusade, I could not believe what had happened to this last remaining stretch of native Florida landscape. The owners of Molasses Swamp had offered to donate the land to the city for a park. But the city leaders' covetous eyes, envious ears, and hardened hearts opted for the tax revenues instead. So the land had been sold, and a bulldozer had a few days before leveled Molasses Swamp for development.

There was no other way to the Talton home except past the "graveyard": huge old-growth trees lying on their sides, dying; hawks flying in circles overhead, screeching in anger and fear; gopher turtles smashed all over the highways, fleeing for their lives from one mechanical monster to be flattened by another; red foxes careening throughout the neighborhood, with no place to go. And all night long I was kept awake by the whippoorwills, which cried out in pain, their babies killed, their homes destroyed, their lives in Naples, Florida, over.

In the kitchen of the Talton home I found a picture of kids gathered in a circle praying in front of one of the small lakes of what was once Molasses Swamp. When I asked when this was taken, Martha Talton told how the night before the bulldozers came, she gathered her daughter and her daughter's friends together. They walked to Molasses Swamp, where they played one last time. Just before they left it for the last time, they joined in a circle, thanked God for the gift of this magical spot of Earth, and then as a final act of love, threw some flowers into the water.

We must come apart so we don't come apart and lose eyes to see, ears to hear, hearts to break.

CHAPTER NINE

Embrace the Unknown

O ne of the major causes of stress in life is uncertainty, dealing with the unknown. Jesus loves surprises. Jesus loves the surprises of God, and the surprises of life when doing the will of God. Jesus is a master of the unknown.

On two occasions in the Gospels Jesus expressly registers surprise, for opposite reasons. In the first, Jesus is surprised because of his hometown's unbelief (Mark 6:6). The second occasion is on account of the Roman soldier's belief (Luke 7:9). Jesus uses the metaphor of surprise to describe the kingdom of God—it is like finding a treasure hidden in a field, it is like discovering that pearl of great value you've always dreamed about, to name but two examples.

The entire gospel of Jesus the Christ is fundamentally a gospel of surprise, filled with unexpected stories, unexpected playmates, unexpected metaphors, unexpected disciples.[1] Jesus surprises people with the place of his hometown. He surprises people with his teachings (Mark 1:22) and his unconventional table seatings (Luke 14:10). Jesus surprises people with his love for metaphors and his preferred manner of teaching—parables (Mark 6:2). Jesus surprises everyone with the residents of his new temple in which God might dwell, "a community of the unexpected"[2] gathered from the byways and back-alleys, from the highways and hedgerows.

Jesus surprises his contemporaries by holding up as models of goodness people who do not agree with him and people who choose not to follow him (for example, the Samaritan). Jesus surprises everyone by celebrating truth wherever he finds it. It is a surprise pick of places and ways for Jesus to die. And the biggest surprise in all of history? The resurrection three days later.

As a child in Pittsburgh, Annie Dillard tells how she used to hide a "precious penny" for someone to find. She would do this just for the fun of it. Sometimes she would even draw with chalk big arrows on the sidewalk, cluing strangers to the "Money This Way" or "Surprise Ahead." Then she would watch from her hiding place, waiting for some anonymous passerby, anyone at all, to find her "free gift from the universe." She concludes by observing that "the world is fairly studded and strewn" with lucky pennies flung everywhere from God's generous hand.[3]

"Adults" learn that surprises, empty schedules, and unpredictability make people nervous. Indeed, surprise is

> **No tears for the writer, no tears for the reader. No surprise for the writer, no surprise for the reader.**
>
> *Robert Frost*

> **The hint half guessed, the gift half understood, is Incarnation.**
>
> *T. S. Eliot*[4]

the enemy of preference and promotion. Hence the growing number of "McChurches" where quality control insures no one will ever be surprised and everything is comfortable and explained.

Privately, the Bible says Jesus may have explained everything (Mark 4:34), but his disciples often understood nothing. Jesus was not an answer-machine spitting out answers to everything. He did not answer everything asked of him (see his exchange with Pilate, for example). In Jesus' mind "Knowing All need not mean Telling All."[5] Jesus spoke truths that left more to be said. He entrusted his life and his death to a loving God, ready to be surprised by whatever God purposed for him.

> ## The unexpected is the gift of God.
>
> *Petru Dumitriu,*
> *Poet and mystic*

One of the reasons why cities are in such trouble is that they were so heavily planned, laid out, rationalized, and neat that they wiped out the gift of "surprise" that makes a city so charming—the magic of the chance encounter you can find lurking behind the mundane, the quirky around-the-corner "what-is-this?", the random flourish of detail, the sudden roofscape, the obscure nook. Richard Sennett, describing the quest for "the purified community" that dominated the psychology of urban planners, says that "Their impulse has been to give way to that tendency, developed in adolescence, of men to control unknown threats by eliminating the possibility for experiencing surprise."[6]

Jesus opened himself to the serendipitous future, to the random, to the surprising, to the strange. Like every Jewish prophet before him, Jesus could both see where he was going and yet be surprised by how God got him there and by what he found when he got there. Jesus taught that only when we give ourselves away, and open our outlooks and obsessions to the mysteries of the Spirit, can we be truly alive.

In Jesus' last words, he committed his life and death into God's hands— "Into your hands I commend my spirit" (Luke 23:46)—to be satisfied with, to be surprised by, the mysterious will of God. Is this not one reason why we fear death so much—we fear surprises? There are two certainties about death. First, death will be full of surprises. Second, it will be a coming into an inheritance.

> *If you want to make God laugh, tell him your plans.*
>
> John Chancellor,
> *Former news anchor*

Can anyone tell what one day will bring forth, much less one month or one year or one lifetime? The laws of quantum theory are stranger than one can imagine. Strangeness is built into the very essence of life. If you're not open to surprises, then you're not open to other people. Nor can you be open to the future. This is one reason why some of history's greatest innovators in one area appear so antediluvian in another. Luther, for example, was open to surprises and new ways of thinking in the realm of theology. But in the realm of astronomy he pulled down the shades on surprise. He thought his neighbor Copernicus was a stark-raving lunatic.

Novelist Fay Weldon created a character whose motto was: "If you do the unexpected, unexpected things happen." Conversely, if you go through life only doing the expected, expected things happen. Paradoxically, one of the chief ways of dealing with stress is to invite some chaos into your life.

> **Keep watch, because you do not know on what day your Lord will come.**
>
> *(Matt. 24:42 NIV)*

When the history of Western civilization is one day written, one of its greatest achievements will no doubt be seen to be its high levels of health. "Modern medicine" and its clinical models made tremendous strides by breaking down the body into specialties, emphasizing the functioning of the parts over the synergy of the whole.

But even "modern medicine" is having to come to terms with the fact that it can no longer see the universe as cause-and-effect. And the medical community is taking great strides in understanding the body "connectionally" as a system of interdependent and interpenetrating parts that relate in unpredictable ways. When things are allowed to interact, complexity theory teaches us, they will evolve variety and the synergy of surprise.

In chaotic systems, physicists tell us "chaos" is not random, as we have been trained to think of "chaos." Rather, chaos has regularities and patterns, but these regularities and patterns cannot be reduced to linear equations or predictable outcomes. Meteorologists can't predict the weather, not because they can't "read" the screens properly, or they don't have enough information to base analysis, or their computers aren't powerful enough. Meteorologists can't positively "forecast" the future because chaotic systems like weather, or like life, have surprise built into their very essence. Even robots are no longer designed to follow slavishly their programming; they are being conditioned to cope with the unexpected ("fuzzy computers" they're called).

I seldom watch the Tournament of Roses parades, but one of the

> **The world may not only be stranger than we suppose, it may be stranger than we can suppose.**
>
> *J. B. S. Haldane*

few years I did (1983) I shall never forget one float in particular. The theme for the year was "Rejoice," and a float appeared on the television screen named "Rejoice Anyway." It featured a mother goose with several little goslings hatching from their shells.

But one shell opened to reveal, not a gosling, but an alligator. Have any alligators been slithering into your life? You expect goslings, but you get alligators? Does life always work out as you hope? Can you rejoice anyway, even when alligators replace goslings?

Over and over again Jesus disconcerted his followers by risking the unknown, hosting new thoughts, and generally allowing the unforeseen and unpredictable entrance into his life. Perhaps he learned this openness to the surprises of God's Spirit from table conversations where he heard his parents tell how the surprise gifts of gold, frankincense, and myrrh financed the family's flight into Egypt to escape the Herod decree. However he learned to expect surprises from God, Jesus calls us to be his SOUL sisters and brothers, as Bruce Larson phrases it—S(ervants) O(f an) U(npredictable) L(ord).[7]

There is an imaginative enfranchisement involved in risking. The world of the quantum is emergent, spontaneous, causal, and creative. A quantum-based consciousness facilitates surprise. Physicist Freeman Dyson argues that "the great task before us now, as citizens of the world, is to learn to organize our societies in such a way that unpredictable things have a chance to happen."[8] One of the reasons we need to get out-of-doors into nature is because there is where the unknown happens, there is where we encounter surprise, there is where we most readily experience the magic of the moment.

Jesus embraced the unknown, risked living on "the edge of chaos," and in taking risks he opened windows to the wonders of eternity. During the modern era westerners said good-bye to one another by this favorite sign-off: "Take Care." In the postmodern era a better sign-off might be: "Take Risks." Or best of all, new paradigm leaders could take their good-byes by saying: "Take Care: Take Risks: Take Compassion." As the philosopher William James put it:

"It is only by risking our persons from one hour to another that we live at all. And often enough our faith beforehand in an uncertified result is the only thing that makes the result come true."[9]

I

A Sufi story tells of an island somewhere and its inhabitants. These islanders longed to move to another land where they could have a healthier and better life. The problem was that the practical arts of swimming and sailing had never been developed—or were lost long before. For that reason, there were some people who simply refused to think of alternatives to life on the island, whereas others intended to seek a solution to their problems locally, without any thought of crossing the waters. From time to time, some islanders reinvented the arts of swimming and sailing. Also from time to time a student would come up to them, and the following exchange would take place:

> "I want to learn to swim [so I can go to another land]."
> "Do you want to make a bargain about it?"

In Seattle the Wizz-Kids, a softball team made up of kidney and liver transplant recipients, beat the Heartbeats, a team of heart transplant recipients, in a game that turned on several close calls by the umpires, all cornea transplant recipients.[10]

"No, I only have to take my ton of cabbages."

"What cabbage?"

"The food which I will need on the other island."

"There is better food there."

"I don't know what you mean. I cannot be sure. I take my cabbage."

"You cannot swim, for one thing, with a ton of cabbage. [It's too much weight.]"

"Then I cannot go [or learn how to swim]. You call it a load. I call it my essential nutrition."

"Suppose, as an allegory, we say not 'cabbage,' but 'assumptions,' or 'destructive ideas'?"

"I am going to take my cabbage to some instructor who understands my needs."[11]

One of the areas in which most scholars are agreed, is that Jesus performed feats that at the time would have been classified as "miracles." Josephus, writing near the end of the first century, admitted that Jesus was known as "a doer of startling deeds."

As much as Jesus loved surprises, and employed his wonder-working powers to startle people into higher and deeper dimensions of living, Jesus seemed acutely aware that "miracles" can be easily misunderstood. He refused to produce miracles on demand (see him before Pilate), and he was reluctant to use them to validate his ministry (Luke 7:18-23), especially since the works of the devil can also be seen as "miraculous" (Mark 3:22). At one point Jesus turned away from his ministry of healing, not because it was failing, but because it was working too well. When Jesus saw that people were coming to him for cures but not for conversion, he put a finger to his lips about the miracles.

In fact, Jesus could sometimes appear as a downright skeptic when it came to the spiritual celebrities of the hour—the necromancers, the gurus, the magicians. On more than one occasion Jesus commands silence about his miracles, and on one occasion he cries out in anger: "It is a wicked, godless generation that asks for a sign" (Matt. 12:39 REB). In Mark 8:11-12, Jesus absolutely refuses to give a sign. Few things provoke the anger of Jesus quite so much as the corruption of the Temple.

Postmodern culture is nowhere near so reluctant. We have rediscovered miracles. In 1991 eight out of ten Americans said they believe in miracles, and a 1994 Gallup/*USA Today*/CNN poll confirmed the stability of the figure, with 76 percent believing in angels.[12] Postmodern culture has been called a "fantastic" culture with a deep "hunger for wonders," in constant "search of the miraculous."[13] The concept of "fantastic," according to Todorov's definition, points to a world where events have rational explanations, but where irrational and suprarational explanations also fit the facts, and seem in some respects even more compelling. Postmoderns are less inclined to dismiss God's wonders than in the modern era. They have little trouble identifying with William Cowper, who on the eve of his second suicide attempt wrote "God moves in mysterious ways his wonders to perform."

> ### The only reason I led the NBA in rebounding was because I got a lot of help from my teammates—they did a lot of missing.
>
> *Moses Malone,*
> *Basketball star*

For the church fathers of the first five centuries, this was precisely the definition of a miracle: "anything that evokes our wonder." According to church historian Rowan A. Greer, a miracle was "an indication of the divine and not something contrary to nature, irrational or superstitious."[14] The miracles of Jesus' day were "worlds removed from magic," according to another church historian, "which is often practiced in an atmosphere of fear, anxiety, and even death. Miracles are performed in an atmosphere of faith, love, conversion, and life."[15]

By contrast, the church operates most often by the Sherlock

Holmes method, which is to exclude everything that is impossible, and then whatever is left must be truth. This may solve crime mysteries, but not divine mysteries and life mysteries.

> *The responsibility of power is like holding an egg. Grasp it too tightly and it will drip through your fingers; hold it too loosely and it will drop and break.*
>
> *Ashanti proverb*

A dignified, dog-collared pastor was visiting a nursing home where a parishioner who used a wheelchair lived. As he stood to leave, he took her hand gently and prayed a sweet, simple prayer. He asked God to be with her, to bring her comfort and strength and healing.

When he finished praying, the woman's face began to glow. Her countenance began to grow brighter and brighter. Suddenly she said, "Pastor, would you help me to my feet?" Not knowing what else to do, he helped her up. At first she halted, then took a few faltering steps. Then she began to jump up and down, then to shout and dance, to cry and praise God until the whole nursing home came alive with energy.

The minister hurried red-faced out to his car, closed the door, grabbed hold of the steering wheel, and with trembling voice uttered this prayer: "Lord, don't you ever do that to me again!"[16]

How ironic that the church is reluctant to claim its own alternative healing methods when there is growing openness to alternative healing. In any year, one in three USAmericans try some kind of alternative medicine, according to a survey published in the 1993 *New England Journal of*

Medicine.[17] Americans made 425 million visits to practitioners of alternative medicine in 1990, and paid more than $14 billion for the care they received—only a fraction of which is covered by insurance. Types of alternative therapies include: diet/nutritional—macrobiotics, megavitamins, diets, lifestyle changes; and mind-body control—relaxation techniques, art therapy, biofeedback, meditation, guided imagery, hypnotherapy, sound/music, deep breathing.

The medical establishment is starting to get the message. Medical schools like Harvard, Stanford, and Georgetown are offering courses in alternative medicine—or what some physicians prefer to call "complementary care." There is even a new branch of the National Institutes of Health called The Office of Alternative Medicine (OAM), thanks to former Iowa Representative Berkley Bedell, who introduced the bill that created it into Congress.

How ironic and tragic that the church still finds the very concept of miracles distasteful in a day when Paul Simon sings "These are the days of miracles and wonder"; when Bernie Siegel writes a blockbuster book called *Love, Medicine and Miracles* (1986); when *Life* magazine asks in its

> *A hospital clinic for hypochondriacs will open next month in Bergen, Norway. The idea is to help people who suffer from ailments that they don't really have. Thus, only patients in good health will be admitted.*
>
> New York Times,
> *February 1995*

July 1991 cover story "Do You Believe in Miracles?"; when the Christmas 1992 motto of the American Foundation for AIDS Research is: "Miracles Happen"; when Gallup reveals that eight of ten USAmericans believe God performs miracles; when Mary sightings are on the rise; and when books on angels are enjoying celestial sales.

Part of the appeal of New Agers is their head start in reclaiming and exploring the landscape of healing, prodigies, miracles, mysteries, signs, and wonders.[18] Jean Houston is out there giving sellout workshops on "The Path of Joy: Miracles, Musicals, and the Laughter of the Gods." Even academics are integrating the unknown and mysterious into their personal credos. Mircea Eliade was a master of vast fields—anthropology, history of religions, orientalism, ritual studies, psychology, novels. Here is the astonishing "confession" by one of the giant intellects of the twentieth century:

> *I do not personally believe there is such a thing as a "random" event. "Unpredictable" is a factual description; "random" contains, without having the honesty to admit it, a philosophical bias typical of persons who have forgotten how to pray. . . . I must now openly state my own bias and say that I do not believe in Chance; I believe in Providence and Miracles.*
>
> *W. H. Auden*[19]

In a "world" composed of billions of galaxies, including, quite probably, a million inhabited planets . . . all the classical arguments for or against the existence of God seem to me naïve and even childish. I do not think that, for the moment, we have the right to argue philosophically. The problem should be left in suspension as it is. We must content ourselves with personal certitudes, with wagers based on dreams, with divinations, ecstasies, aesthetic emotions. That also is a mode of knowing, but without arguments.[20]

Karin Granberg-Michaelson, in her book *Healing Community* (1991), poses questions for every new paradigm leader and community:

- Are we and our churches healing communities?
- Are we really engaging ourselves in God's controversy with those who spread sickness around?
- Are we enabling our sick people and societies to diagnose their true sickness and find resources for healing?
- Are we prepared to place ourselves beside the sick, the deprived, the oppressed with the healing power of God?
- Are we ready to join our Lord in his self-giving struggle with evil even to the cross in order that healing, reconciliation, and wholeness may become manifest in a world which is sick unto death?[21]

The symbolism of "oil"—which today sends us to do battle in the world (planes, tanks, ships) or in the workplace (cars) and is literally *exhausting* our earth to death—will be invested with new meaning through healing and anointing rituals, both the oil of healing and the oil of health (or "gladness"). Bible studies, prayers for the sick, laying on of hands, anointings, holy communion, healing liturgies, music ministries (just as medicine works healing in the body, so music works healing in the soul) are but a few of the ritual activities churches can use. Christ Church in Memphis, for example, has a weekly Sunday night "healing" service, and puts out a pamphlet entitled "A Ministry of Healing and Wholeness," which gives a theological rationale for the healing services, their "laying on of hands," and anointing with oil.

II

A world full of hype, a world empty of hope, is desperately scanning the horizon for a word that will bring wonder and spark back into its chin-draggin', soul-saggin', heart-laggin' life. "A miracle is a 'sign' occasionally sent to us from the promised land, like an interstellar light that gives us a glimpse of undreamt wonders."[22] Many years ago, after lecturing on miracles in a German seminary, the great theologian Karl Rahner was asked this question by a seminarian: "Can you give us a specific example of a miracle?" Dr. Rahner replied: "There is only one miracle: Life."

Life is God's ultimate miracle. The heart of soul is mystery. Religious faith deepens and widens the mysteries; it does not banish them. The resurrection doesn't solve the puzzle. The resurrection deepens the mystery.

A two-year-old boy named Thane Phelan Sweet taught his parents this lesson one Christmas. When the crèche was put up, Thane became quite enchanted by the baby Jesus lying in the manger. So enchanted, in fact, that Thane kept stealing baby Jesus from the manger and hiding him at various locations around the house. Thane's parents never knew where baby Jesus would turn up after he was found missing.

One time he was found in the kitchen, in a manger of spoons in the utensil drawer. Another time something fell out of the Christmas tree, and when Thane's parents went to investigate, sure enough, it was baby Jesus amid the presents. One morning Thane's father went to put on his shoes, only to awaken baby Jesus with his toes.

No amount of parental entreaties to "Leave baby Jesus where he belongs" could deter Thane from his self-appointed mission of finding new surprise places to stash the Savior. In fact, when Thane deemed his parents too slow in discovering where he had taken baby Jesus, he helped them out by placing baby Jesus in the middle of the floor for immediate discovery.

How many of us are uncomfortable with a God who is full of surprises, a God who is constantly showing up in unexpected places, a Christ-Spirit who cannot be confined to where we want to keep him?

One hesitates to speak with authority on scarcely speakable things like miracles, but this one thing I know. Don't believe in miracles. Count on them.

CHAPTER TEN

✳ ✳ ✳
Moodle Along the Way
✳ ✳ ✳

You say you never heard of "moodling"? Have you ever heard of "jazz"? The great trumpet player Louis Armstrong was lecturing to a college music workshop on his training, his technique, his repertoire, his armature, when a young student inserted this question: "Mr. Armstrong, what really *is* jazz?" Armstrong thought for a moment, and then, with a touch of sympathy in his voice, replied: "Man, if you gotta ask you'll never know." According to *Codex Bezae* (D), Jesus once said something similar to the people of his day: "On the same day, he saw a man working on the Sabbath and said to him, Man, if you know what you are doing, you are blessed; but if you do not know, you are accursed."[1]

If you gotta ask what "moodling" is, you ain't got it. Moodling is a very simple name given to a very complex phenomenon. Perhaps it is better described than defined: lying in the shade under a tree by a lake, watching the clouds roll by; sitting in a hot tub, letting your thoughts flow; sleeping in a hammock under a harvest moon; riding horseback through a field; lollygagging on your walk home; marveling in a garden.

There is a *Frank and Ernest* cartoon that has the two of them riding a road that is marked by an arrow "Road to Success." But up ahead is another sign: "Be Prepared to Stop."

> ***If we had a keen vision of all that is ordinary in human life, it would be like hearing the grass grow or the squirrel's heart beat, and we should die of that roar which is the other side of silence.***
>
> *George Eliot*[2]

In a world that prizes bigness, we need to be reminded that small is beautiful. In a world that worships speed, we need to be reminded that slow is beautiful. Stop is beautiful. Sabbath is beautiful. Moodling is beautiful. An old proverb goes like this:

> Fear less: hope more
> Eat less: chew more
> Whine less: breathe more
> Talk less: say more
> Hate less: love more
> And all good things will be yours.

A healthy lifestyle is comprised of causal time, when one makes a difference, and pausal time, when one reflects on what kind of difference one is making. Whether it was the first-century equivalent of a ten-minute siesta, or a gardenia bubble bath, Jesus knew the meaning of pausal time. Jesus meandered and mulled. In current jargon, Jesus knew how to relax.

Jesus moodled. And Jesus offers to teach us how to moodle.

"Come to me, all you that are weary and are carrying heavy burdens, and I will give you rest" (Matt. 11:28).

The church may translate the last word in that verse "work," but the first thing Jesus offers us is a place to stop, a place of pausal time, a place where we can find "rest for our soul." For everyone who is misplaced, whether down and out or up and out, for everyone who is living a displaced life, Jesus offers us a place to stop.

Joseph Campbell in his famous PBS interview with Bill Moyers confessed that most of his friends were living "Wasteland Lives." He said that they are "just baffled; they're wandering in the wasteland without any sense of where the water is—the Source that makes things green."

Not long after I heard this exchange I was reading Tom Wolfe's novel *The Bonfire of the Vanities*, where one of the leading characters, successful Wall Street bond broker Sherman McCoy, finds everything he has worked so hard to put together falling apart when he is accused of a hit-and-run accident.

> **He that believeth shall not make haste.**
>
> *(Isa. 28:16 KJV)*

Stung by the pain of desertion in his hour of public exposure, he says to his lawyer, "It's . . . sobering how fast it goes when it goes . . . all these ties you have, all these people you went to school with and to college, the people who are in your clubs, the people you go out to dinner with—it's all a thread . . . all these ties that make up your life, and when it breaks . . . that's it . . . that's it."[3]

Joseph Campbell and Thomas Wolfe are right. It doesn't matter how vast your portfolio, how numerous your Club Med packages, or how full your closets are with designer clothes. However individualized and customized fears become, the fears and facts are the same for everyone: the fear of being used; the fear of growing old; the fear of losing health and home; the fear of being left alone; the fear of dying; the fact of loneliness; the fact of rejection; the fact of emptiness; the fact of tiredness. However lovely the surface of things may be, there is anguish below for everyone.

Whether you are living wasteland lives or wasted lives, whether you are maxed out on materialism or zoned out on drugs, Christ offers a place to stop, a place where you can go to warm your poor and cold soul, a place to explore the feeling that "there has to be more to life than this," a place to examine your scattered, battered life and ask what kind of race you are running, a place to hit the pause button . . .

> a place to ponder why when you reach the top you often hit rock bottom;
> a place to get off the carousel of greater and greater means and less and less meaning;
> a place to pick up the pieces after slamming into the wall of mortality;
> a place to climb down from the ladder that helps you reach enough to live by and puts you on the elevator that lifts you up to reach enough to live for;
> a place to conquer the "Ol' Man River" syndrome— "feared of living and scared of dyin' ";
> a place to escape the paid hacks and flacks who would have you believe that a beer or a date is as good as it gets;
> a place to ponder why those who work with the frailest and neediest in our society are paid the least, not the most;
> a place to discover that somebody is stealing from you; somebody is stealing the most precious thing you've got; somebody is stealing your life;
> a place to realize that you can make millions of dollars and still flunk life;
> a place to explore the difference between the right to do your own thing and doing the right thing;
> a place to look at things from the inside out;
> a place to cut the chains of runaway thoughts and

> fears run riot that are keeping you on the
> treadmill—"I'm shy," "It runs in the family,"
> "I'm a born pessimist," "I can never change,"
> "I'm no good," "No one loves me," "I'm
> trapped."

A place to stop is important. Moodling is vital to a healthy lifestyle and a healthy spirituality.

One of my favorite places in the whole world to work is the Union League Club of Chicago. Amid world-class art and museum-quality antiques, Robert Nelson (I call him my guru) tutors me in the art of fund- and friend-raising. The first time he sent me to make a phone call to a prospective donor, I went over to a bank of phone booths off the main dining room, sat down, and tried to get the light to come on. Try as I might, I could find no switch. In exasperation more than in embarrassment, I returned to Bob's table and said, "How do you get the light to come on?"

"You're the head of a seminary?" he muttered in apparent delight. "Did you try closing the door?"

Sure enough, the lights came on once I first closed the door. Lights don't come on unless you first shut some doors. Life doesn't come into focus unless you first stop. If your life doesn't have an "off" switch, it will never turn on. Moodling is taking the time "off" to experience lightenings. . . . Yes, there is more to life—and Jesus is where you find it. Here is the beginning of a new life:

> What is your deepest treasure?
> God is.
> The treasure is within you.
> The treasure is not without you.

Thomas Moore tells of how "sometimes in their chanting, monks will land upon a note and sing it in florid fashion, one syllable of text for fifty notes of chant. Melisma, they call it. Living a melismatic life in imitation of plainchant, we may stop on an experience, a place, a person, or a memory and rhapsodize in imagination. Some like to meditate or contemplate melismatically, while others prefer to draw, build, paint, or dance whatever their eye has fallen upon. Living one point after another is one form of experience, and it can be emphatically productive. But stopping for melisma gives the soul its reason for being."[4]

Jesus stopped for melisma. Jesus moodled. And Jesus calls us to moodle.

"Moodling" doesn't mean Jesus got enough sleep, although it can mean that. Even though God needed to relax one day a week, many of us think we are better than God. Many of us operate with the policy of one of my summer employers: "If you're well enough to call in sick, Sweet, you're well enough to come to work."

Jesus functioned along different lines. He knew when he needed to draw breath. He knew when it was time for his mindbodyspirit to recuperate, to rejuvenate, to recreate. He knew when to moodle, and coast along in a state of reverence and reverie rather than intellection and control. He was in such little hurry that he conversed with strangers while drawing water at wells (John 4:1-26). He frequently "cut a firebreak" in his schedule to admire the lilies of the field (Matt. 6:28) or to watch a sunrise or sunset (Matt. 5:45 and 14:23). He built in desert "downtime" to pray (Luke 5:16) and to vacation with friends (Mark 8:27). So that his soul could catch up with his body, he spent a whole night in prayer (Luke 6:12). Jesus learned how to cultivate the art of nonthinking, the art of silence.

> *I shan't get well unless I go and lie down on my bed. I never was well except lying down on the Universe.*
>
> *Poet Fernando Pessoa*[5]

A cartoon depicts three priests in a sanctuary. They hear a voice, and see some lights high at the other corner of the cathedral. One of them says, "I think maybe it's the second coming." Another exclaims: "What do we do?" The third says, "Look busy."

Jesus didn't always look busy. He didn't always have something to do. He didn't always have something to say. In fact, Jesus spent a great deal of time doing absolutely nothing. If he had nothing to do, he did it.

For example, Jesus didn't hide his napping, like some presidents have tried to do. He could sleep anywhere, any time, even in a boat about to capsize (remember the story of Jesus snoozing on a pillow in the back of the boat during the storm in Mark 4:38?). He believed that in some situations a siesta was the most spiritual thing one could do.

Or say nothing. Sometimes silence is more spiritual than speech. Derek Raymond, in his autobiography *The Hidden Files* (1992) says that "Even before I get there I can see that hell is going to be a noisy place. Like a pub, it is designed to cover interior silence; whereas happiness I think reveals silence as the best thing."[6]

The new historicism and postmodern literary criticism attends carefully to the significance of silences—what is absent is often as revealing as what is present. All the great religions of the world have spaces of silence or buffer zones—equivalents of the weekly "Seventh Day" and yearly "Lent." In the Jewish-Christian tradition, the point of the Sabbath is less its usefulness as a day of rest so that we can be better able to work the other six days, but more its uselessness as a day of doing nothing to remind us that God is God and we are not. We need constant reinforcement that the world does not revolve around you or me or depend upon our labor.

No one has expressed the paradox of moodling any better than the Argentinean writer Antonio Porchia: "A full heart has room for everything and an empty heart has room for nothing. Who understands?"[7] Like that proverbial old gentleman, "Sometimes I sits and reads, sometimes I sits and thinks, and sometimes, Ah jest sits." Or as one of the burned-out younger brothers in the movie *Mac* complained to an overbearing older brother who insisted they work seven days a week, "Even the sun doesn't come out every day."

Love and compassion must sometimes give way to hygiene. Evelyn Underhill once observed how some Christians "desert God by entering his service instead." Leslie Weatherhead said much the same thing, but more poignantly: "God wants your heart not your heartiness." Paul likewise talks about those who still have the form of religion but have lost its force. God calls us to burn up in service—not burn out. We can burn up without burning out only by moodling—by giving our souls their proper care and feeding.

Nazarene preacher Bob Benson tells of his custom of never going to bed without kissing his kids, whether they are awake or asleep. "One night I bent over and kissed Patrick on the cheek and quickly stood up and started out of the room. I was so tired I thought it was about the last 'get up' I had left for the whole day, when his question stopped me cold and brought me back to his bedside. 'Why do you kiss me so fast?' "[8]

Why do we let the most precious moments of life go by so fast? Why do we kiss the best things in life so hurriedly? Ecologists are calling for a worldwide ceremonial "Stop Everything Week" that would shut down the engines that drive this consumer society—so that we could "kiss the joy" more, and draw breath. Planet Earth as well needs to draw breath and be kissed.

> *[Scipio was] never less idle than when wholly idle, nor less alone than when wholly alone.*
>
> Cicero's beginning to his *Third Book of* De Officiis

Indeed, the postmodern world is open to "ceremony" precisely because it is ceremony that forces it to slow down and slacken its frantic pace of living. The church must craft new liturgies that can be woven into the warp and woof of every corner of life, liturgies that instruct us in methods of living known best by the lilies—"they toil not, neither do they spin."

II

By the "art of moodling" is meant most deeply this: Jesus did not always bring life under his control. He didn't swim twenty-four hours a day. He understood the mystery of floating. He didn't just swim through life, or poise his body for the big wave. Jesus spent a lot of time floating. Or as one person put it after I presented some of this material in a lecture, "You know why Jesus walked on water, preacher? He probably didn't even know *how* to swim."

Disciples of Jesus need to learn to float. We're either incurable landlubbers or we're inveterate swimmers. We don't want to let go and relinquish ourselves to the water and waves. We want to go where *we* want to go, and are not about to let the water and waves take us where they would have us go.

We are heavy into control. In fact, if the truth be told, we are control junkies, hooked to the illusion of being "in control." In my lectures to students, I sometimes have them take a spiritual biopsy of the heart of the modern and postmodern eras by comparing one of the favored ways moderns traversed the waters (powerboat) versus the characteristically postmodern use of the kayak, which has become one of the most popular ways people today strike out for the wide open water places.

In powerboat "top-down" modes of thought and nodes of knowledge, you are elevated above the water and protected from it. You look down on the environment through which you are passing. Clearly, in these kids' bathtub boats on steroids, you are in control. But the price for that heady control is high: There is heavy wastage and pollution of both sound and energy. The powerboat is an example *de luxe* of the paradox of modern attempts at "objectivity": doing in-depth work from a distance.

By contrast, the coffin-boat kayak is without glitz, gadgets, and dazzle. But its "bottom-up" approach doesn't disturb the world it's in. Indeed, to kayak you must become a marine mammal yourself. You put on a silly "skirt"; you get wet and dirty; you don't ride "on" the water, you ride "in" the water as you eyeball nature, without shock absorbers, on an equal basis. How

> ### Control doesn't work.
>
> *James C. Collins and
> William C. Lazier,
> Stanford management theorists[9]*

"expert" you become depends, not on the horsepower of your machine, but upon your ability to read the moods and motions of the wind and water, and to work with your environment.

The safest way to voyage is in groups of two boats or more, where there is wide individual freedom within the context of a tight team dominated by a spirit of camaraderie, cooperation, and mutual dependence. In kayaking, there is no wastage or pollution, and the silence transmutes the soul into the transcendent.

If sea kayaking or white-water rafting is one of the best metaphors to convey what it is like to live in a postmodern world, then we had better learn the "Five Rules of White-water Rafting" as found on the Snake River in Idaho. I call these "Life's Five Spiritual Laws" (when slightly altered):

1. Go with the flow, and don't get addled. (Translate: Go with the Spirit, and have no fear.)
2. Lean into the rocks. Rocks are your friends.
3. Feet first, toes out, when you go into the turbulence.

4. If worse comes to worse, let go of everything and eventually you'll come up.

5. You're here because of the danger, so enjoy it.

To mix metaphors: The Scriptures teach that the spirit "blows where it wills." To live in the Spirit is to ride the winds, and let the winds of God's Spirit blow through us until we become God's instruments of play, sounding the music of the spheres and their songs of purest praise. As the Holy Ghost moved upon the waters, only those things that were movable were formed into things for God. It is only what is movable and malleable that the Holy Ghost can use to make Christ known. Are we movable and malleable for God? Are we or is God "in control" of our lives?

Aside from the not inconsequential fact that Newtonian assumptions of predictability and control are gone (which is a subject for quite another book), there is something even deeper. God has so structured the moral universe that the best things of life don't happen when we're "in control." How many people have fallen in love when they were "in control"? How many of life's best moments occur when you're "in control"?

The hardest things to learn in life are when to be rigid and when to relax; when to bring things to order or when to live with chaos; when to be stiff and stubborn or when to be loose and pliant; when to make things happen and when to let things happen; when to hold on and stay in there and when to let go and move on; when to change the world to suit our purposes and when to accept the world that suits its own purposes; when to change the situation and when to leave the situation; when to live out of regularities, and when to open up to spontaneities; when to take charge of life and swim against the tide, and when to surrender one's will to the sea, trusting the tide to take one safely home; when to move and when to moodle.

Life is not one big float, or one perpetual free fall. But neither is life one long marathon, one big swim. It is not necessary to always have to whack the rock to get the water out.

Sometimes just a word or a cup under a spout will do. In the words of Jesuit theologian Thomas Green:

> The secret of floating is in learning *not* to do all the things we instinctively want to do. . . . We want to keep our heads out of the water to avoid having our noses and mouths filled with the sea, but the more we raise our heads, the more likely we are to be unbalanced and to end up with a noseful of water. If we can persuade ourselves to put our heads back, to rest on the water as on a pillow, we don't sink; we float![10]

The water is a symbol of chaos. Faith is learning that you are part of the sea that is God, a sea that is powerful, uncontrollable, always changing and always leading to new complexities. Faith is also trusting the God who created the waters, even giving ourselves to the waters in trust of the God who holds us and carries us. Faith is our ability to trust Christ with our lives as we trust the water with our bodies. The water will carry you. Christ will not let you down. It is easy to trust God too little. It is difficult to trust God too much.

We should never give up in life. But we should sometimes give in, and let go to the flow of life. To dare a paraphrase of poet John Ashbery's line "Sometimes you get lost. But life knows where you are."[11]

Sometimes you get lost. But God knows where you are.

O Jesus,

Be the canoe that holds me up in
the sea of life;

Be the rudder that keeps me in
the straight road;

Be the outrigger that supports me
in times of temptation,

Let your Spirit be my sail that
carries me through each day.

Keep my body strong, so I can
paddle steadfastly on
in the voyage of life. Amen.

An islander's prayer from Melanesia[12]

The Code of Healthy Living

1. "A Nation of the Quick and the Dead-Tired," *Newsweek*, 6 March 1995, 3, and Lyn-Nell Hancock with Debra Rosenberg and others, "Breaking Point," *Newsweek*, 56-62.
2. Robert Anderson, *Stress Power: How to Turn Tension into Energy* (New York: Human Sciences Press, 1978), 18.
3. Marcia Mogelonsky, "Cooking from Scratch Goes Full Speed," *American Demographics*, March 1995, 15.
4. Juliet B. Schor, *The Overworked American: The Unexpected Decline of Leisure* (New York: Basic Books, 1993).
5. The inspiration for this list came from Diane Loomans with Julia Loomans, *Full Esteem Ahead: 100 Ways to Build Self-Esteem in Children and Adults* (Tiburon, Calif.: H. J. Kramer, 1994), 162.
6. A. E. Harvey, *Jesus and the Constraints of History* (Philadelphia: Westminster Press, 1982), 98-119.
7. Gerd Theissen, in *Sociology of Early Palestinian Christianity* (Philadelphia: Fortress Press, 1978), speaks of "a basic attitude which was free of anxiety, a renewed trust in reality which issues from the figure of Jesus—even down to our own time" (110).
8. Alan Devoe, "Jesus and Little Lord Fauntleroy," *American Mercury*, November 1948, 591.
9. The *Gospel of Thomas* 1 introduces interestingly as the words of the "living Jesus": "Whoever finds the interpretation of these sayings will not experience death." See John Dominic Crossan, ed. *Sayings Parallels: A Workbook for the Jesus Tradition* (Philadelphia: Fortress Press, 1986), 108.
10. In his October 1992 inaugural address as the Heisel Professor of Evangelization and Church Renewal at United Theological Seminary, Howard Snyder noted the delicious irony that one of the greatest postmoderns in history lived in the first century. See Snyder, "The Gospel as Global Good News," *Journal of Theology* 97 (1993): 31. See Paul J. Achtemeier, "The Origin and Function of the Pre-Markan Miracle Catenae," *Journal of Biblical Literature* 90 (1971): 198-221; and Gerd Theissen, *The Miracle Stories of the Early Christian Tradition* (Philadelphia: Fortress Press, 1983). On the historicity of these stories, see René Latourelle, "Authenticité historique des miracles de Jésus: Essai de critériologie," *Gregorianum* 54 (1973): 225-62.

11. In fact, a hymn at Lauds to this day goes like this:

> Be with us, O Archangel,
> called the Medicine of God;
> drive away diseases of the body
> and bring good health to our minds.

See also stanza four of this ninth-century hymn by Rabanus Maurus:

> Send from the heavens Raphael thine archangel,
> Health-bringer blessed, aiding every sufferer,
> That, in thy service, he may wisely guide us,
> Healing and blessing.

("Christ the fair glory," *The Hymnal of the Protestant Episcopal Church in the United States of America* [New York: Oxford University Press, 1973], 123).

12. See Leonard I. Sweet, *Health and Medicine in the Evangelical Tradition* (New York: Crossroad, 1992).

13. While he overstates his case, Morris Maddocks, in his contemporary classic *The Christian Healing Ministry* (London: SPCK, 1990), quotes the verse in Revelation where the healing waters of life flow from "the throne of God and of the Lamb through the middle of the street of the city" (Rev. 22:1-2) to show how "the healing water is now flowing centrally in our churches. The activities of those prayerfully engaged in the healing ministry, once resigned as it were to the side aisles, are now being integrated into the central witness of the Church and are becoming a significant part of its mission" (215).

14. Paul J. Kenkel, "Companies Sweeten Wellness Plans," *Modern Healthcare,* 23 November 1992, 49.

15. The membership of the College of Chaplains, whose services include the certification of chaplains in healthcare fields, has grown from 2,159 in 1992 to 2,800 in 1995. Chaplains can be found in about 70 percent of all hospitals.

16. According to Ramsay MacMullen, "The chief business of religion [in the time of Jesus] was to make the sick well," in *Paganism in the Roman Empire* (New Haven: Yale University Press, 1981), 49; cf. R. M. Grant, *Gods and the One God* (Philadelphia: Westminster Press, 1986), 54-61, 95-98.

17. The Newe Testament, trans. William Tyndale (1525; reprint, London: D. Paradine Developments, 1976), fol. lvviiii.

18. R. D. Laing, "Religious Experience and the Role of Organized Religion," in *The Role of Religion in Mental Health: Papers Presented at a Conference Organized by the National Association for Mental Health in Conjunction with the Institute of Religion and Medicine* (London: National Association for Mental Health, 1967), 57.

19. For the importance of healing rituals, see Jeanne Achterberg, "Ritual: The Foundation for Transpersonal Medicine," *ReVision* 14 (Winter 1992): 158-61.
20. Faith Popcorn, *The Popcorn Report: Faith Popcorn on the Future of Your Company, Your World, Your Life* (New York: Doubleday, 1991), 62.
21. Ibid., 64.
22. Gustavus Emanuel Hiller, *The Christian Family* (Cincinnati: Jennings & Graham, 1907), 154-56.
23. See *Bede's Ecclesiastical History of the English People,* ed. Bertram Colgrave and R. A. B. Mynors (Oxford: Clarendon Press, 1969), 464-69. Herebald, one of the bishop's clergy, was healed and went on to become the abbot of Tynemouth. John of Beverley, one of the most popular of England's native saints, was the bishop of Hexham at the time of this event. He became bishop of York in 705 and died in 721. Additional accounts of St. John's healing powers are recorded by Bede on pp. 460-61, where prayer alone is used, and on pp. 456-59, where St. John cures a lad of a speech impediment while a physician is called in to heal his scabby head. Thanks to M. L. Cameron, *Anglo-Saxon Medicine* (New York: Cambridge University Press, 1993), 20, for pointing me to these references.

1. Laugh a Lot

1. In John R. Kohlenberger III, *The NRSV Concordance Unabridged* (Grand Rapids, Mich.: Zondervan, 1991), the word "joy" appears fifty-seven times in the Second Testament; "weeping," twenty times; "mourning," seven times; "anger," sixteen times; "distress," eleven times; and while "sad" appears twice, "sadness" is not found.
2. As quoted in Russell Watson, "A Lesser Child of God: The Radical Jesus Seminar Sees a Different Christ," *Newsweek,* 4 April 1994, 54.
3. *The Penguin Dictionary of Modern Humorous Quotations,* comp. Fred Metcalf (New York: Viking, 1986), 94.
4. Burton L. Mack, *A Myth of Innocence: Mark and Christian Origins* (Philadelphia: Fortress Press, 1988). See also Jerry Camery-Hoggatt, *Irony in Mark's Gospel: Text and Subtext* (New York: Cambridge University Press, 1992; Paul D. Duke, *Irony in the Fourth Gospel* (Atlanta: John Knox, 1985).
5. "Joy is above all the fruit of having come face to face with a universal and enduring reality to which one can refer," Pierre Teilhard de Chardin, *Writings in Time of War* (New York: Harper & Row, 1968), 124.
6. *The Poems of Coventry Patmore,* ed. Frederick Page (New York: Oxford University Press, 1949), 483.
7. J. Duncan M. Derrett, "The Lucan Christ and Jerusalem," *Zeitschrift für die Neutestamentliche Wissenschaft* 75 (1984): 36-43. His admittedly "painful" English translation that gives a clue to the amount of punning involved goes like this: "[instead of enquiring of Herod's

*wel*fare] tell this hyena (literally 'fox') that after achieving that men be *well* by dis*possessing* demons today and tomorrow, on the third day I do indeed say fare*well*. For it needs must that today, tomorrow, and the third day I *fare* on, for it is unthinkable that a prophet should be undone outside Jerusalem, the *'Possession of Well' "* (42).

8. See Dennis Smith, "The Historical Jesus at Table," in *Society of Biblical Literature 1989 Seminar Papers,* ed. David J. Lull (Atlanta, Ga.: Scholars Press, 1989), 476.

9. L. Paul Trudinger, "An Israelite in Whom There Is No Guile: An Interpretative Note on John 1:45-51," *Evangelical Quarterly* 54 (1982): 117-20.

10. Robert W. Funk, "The Looking-Glass Tree Is for the Birds: Ezekiel 17:22-24; Mark 4:30-32," *Interpretation* 27 (January 1973): 3-9. The quote is on p. 7.

11. Dan Otto Via, Jr., *The Parables: Their Literary and Existential Dimension* (Philadelphia: Fortress Press, 1967), 162-76.

12. John Dominic Crossan, ed. *Sayings Parallels: A Workbook for the Jesus Tradition* (Philadelphia: Fortress Press, 1986), 92.

13. See also for example Jakob Jónsson, *Humour and Irony in the New Testament* (Leiden: Brill, 1985); Paul D. Duke, *Irony in the Fourth Gospel* (Atlanta: John Knox, 1985); James M. Dawsey, *The Lukan Voice: Confusion and Irony in the Gospel of Luke* (Macon, Ga.: Mercer University Press, 1986); Colin Brown, "The Gates of Hell and the Church," in *Church, Word, and Spirit: Historical and Theological Essays in Honor of Geoffrey W. Bromiley,* ed. James E. Bradley and Richard A. Muller (Grand Rapids, Mich.: Eerdmans, 1987), 15-43.

14. Samuel Beckett, *Murphy* (London: John Calder, 1952), 65, as quoted in Stephen D. Moore, *Mark and Luke in Poststructuralist Perspectives: Jesus Begins to Write* (New Haven: Yale University Press, 1992), 83.

15. Moore, *Mark and Luke in Poststructuralist Perspectives,* 83.

16. Even if the wordplay *petros-petra* in Matt. 16:18 were a stylistic embellishment of Matthew, as George Howard argues in "The Meaning of Petros-Petra," *Restoration Quarterly* 10 (1967): 217-21, the early church still heard and recognized their founding scripture as a pun. For a dissenting voice that challenges the ancient consensus that the *petra* of Matt. 16:18 is to be identified with *Petros,* and this Peter is the foundation of the church, see Chrys C. Caragounis, *Peter and the Rock* (New York: Walter de Gruyter, 1990), where the verse is translated: "As tryly as you are Peter, on this rock [of what you have just said, viz. that I am the Christ] I will build my Church" (119).

17. See "Humor and Wit," *The Anchor Bible Dictionary,* ed. David Noel Freedman (New York: Doubleday, 1992) 3:325-33.

18. The best treatment of the demise of satire and humor is Harvey Cox, *The Feast of Fools: A Theological Essay on Festivity and Fantasy* (Cambridge, Mass.: Harvard University Press, 1969).

19. Ishmael Reed, "The Reactionary Poet," in *New and Collected Poems* (New York: Atheneum, 1988), 159.

20. David Steele, *Slow Down, Moses* (Minneapolis: Augsburg, 1990), 9.

21. Lovett H. Weems, Jr., *Church Leadership: Vision, Team, Culture and Integrity* (Nashville: Abingdon Press, 1993), 15. Weems is quoting from William Faulkner, *Light in August* (New York: Modern Library, 1950), 426, where Faulkner character Gail Hightower, a defrocked Presbyterian minister, muses that "that which is destroying the church is not the outward groping of those within it or the inward groping of those without, but the professionals who control it and who have removed the bells from its steeples."

22. Joey Adams, *Live Longer Through Laughter: How to Use a Joke to Save Your Health, Your Mind, Your Marriage, Your Election, Your Party, Your Speech, Your Business, Your Friends* (New York: Stein and Day, 1984), 30.

23. For an illustration of his humor, see Umberto Eco, *Misreadings*, trans. William Weaver (San Diego: Harcourt, Brace, Jovanovich, 1993).

24. Rabo Karabekian in Kurt Vonnegut, *Bluebeard* (New York: Delacorte Press, 1987), 69.

25. For the argument that we feel sad because we cry instead of crying because we feel sad, see William James, "What Is an Emotion?" *Mind* 9 (1884): 188-205.

26. See the pioneering article by William F. Fry, Jr., "The Respiratory Components of Mirthful Laughter," *Journal of Biological Psychology* 19 (1977): 39-50. Also see Donald W. Black, "Laughter," *JAMA: Journal of the American Medical Association* 252 (7 December 1984): 2995-98.

27. See "Twelve Ways to Have More Fun," *University of Texas Lifetime Health Letter*, September 1992, 3.

28. William F. Fry, Jr., "Laughter and Health," *Medical and Health Annual* 1984 (Chicago: Encyclopedia Britannica, 1984), 262.

29. Ronald S. Laura and Bob Wolff, "Not Just for Laughs: Humor Can Relieve Stress and Prolong Life," *Muscle & Fitness* 53 (December 1992): 148-53.

30. As quoted in Tilden Edwards, *Sabbath Time* (Nashville: Upper Room, 1992), 64.

31. Margaret Brodkin, *Every Kid Counts: 31 Ways to Save Our Children* (San Francisco: HarperSanFrancisco, 1993), 17.

32. Norman Cousins, *Anatomy of an Illness as Perceived by the Patient: Reflections on Healing and Regeneration* (New York: Norton, 1979).

33. Kaye Ann Herth, "Laughter: A Nursing RX," *American Journal of Nursing* 84 (1984): 91-92. See also Vera Robinson, *Humor in the Health Professions* (Thorofare, N.J.: Charles B. Slack, 1977).

34. For example, Holiday Inn excluded all interviewees out of a pool of five thousand who smiled fewer than four times during the interview when looking for five hundred people to fill positions for a new facility. As reported in *Communication Briefings*, 12:6 (March 1993): 4.

2. Hang Out with Friends

1. See the chapter on "The Women's Jesus" in *A Land Flowing with Milk and Honey,* by Elisabeth Moltmann-Wendel (New York: Crossroad, 1986), 117-34.
2. Its development is parallel to *feond:* to hate, enemy, evil spirit. See Robert K. Barnhart, *The Barnhart Dictionary of Etymology* (New York: H. W. Wilson Co., 1988), 409, 380.
3. Nicholas Peter Harvey, *Morals and the Meaning of Jesus: Reflections on the Hard Sayings* (Cleveland: Pilgrim Press, 1993), 94.
4. Ibid., 84-85. Harvey writes: "This essentially non-coercive obedience has to be learned, and can only be learned in the testing exercise of the freedom of authentic personhood" (85).
5. In Ivan Illich's *Tools for Conviviality* (New York: Harper & Row, 1973), he argues that friendship and self-limitation are the indispensable ingredients for the good life.
6. Or this alternate text by Charles A. Tindley:

When the storms of life are raging, Stand by me; . . .
When the world is tossing me,
Like a ship upon the sea,
Thou who rulest wind and water,
Stand by me.

In the midst of tribulation, Stand by me; . . .
When the host of hell assail
And my strength begins to fail,
Thou who never lost a battle,
Stand by me.

In the midst of faults and failures, Stand by me; . . .
When I've done the best I can,
And my friends misunderstand,
Thou who knowest all about me,
Stand by me.

In the midst of persecution, Stand by me; . . .
When my foes in war array
Undertake to stop my way,
Thou who saved Paul and Silas,
Stand by me.

When I'm growing old and feeble, Stand by me; . . .
When my life becomes a burden,
And I'm nearing chilly Jordan,
O thou Lily of the Valley,
Stand by me.

"Stand By Me," *The United Methodist Hymnal* (Nashville: The United Methodist Publishing House, 1989), 512.

7. See the *Gospel of Peter* where the criminal whom he befriended defends Jesus against attacks by the mob and experiences their wrath. The crowd, enraged at the thief, leaves his (that is, the thief's) legs unbroken. Friendship created a community of suffering. The crucifixion portrayed in the *Gospel of Peter* shows us a friendship that transcends suffering and shame. On the *Gospel of Peter,* see John Dominic Crossan, *The Cross That Spoke: The Origins of the Passion Narrative* (San Francisco: Harper & Row, 1988), 165-66.

8. Raymond Brown, 13-14 March 1993, Heck Lectures, United Theological Seminary. See also Brown, *The Death of the Messiah: From Gethsemane to the Grave* (New York: Doubleday, 1994), 910-32.

9. The phrase "Time Porn" was coined by Colin McEnroe in the *Hartford Courant.*

10. Pierre Babin, *The NEW ERA in Religious Communication* (Minneapolis: Fortress Press, 1991), 93.

11. See also *Gospel of Thomas* 99, *The Gospel of Thomas: The Hidden Sayings of Jesus,* trans. Marvin Meyer (San Francisco: HarperSanFrancisco, 1992), 61; 2 Clement 9:10-11.

12. Francis Bacon, "Of Friendship," in *The Works of Francis Bacon, Lord Chancellor of England,* a new ed. by Basil Montagu (London: William Pickering, 1835), 1:91.

13. See the review article "Social Relationships and Health," by James S. House, Karl R. Landis, and Debra Umberson citing sixty-two studies that provide "compelling evidence that lack of social relationships constitutes a major risk factor for mortality," *Science,* 29 July 1988, 540-50. The quote is found on p. 541. Also see the summary review of recent findings in "Social Support: How Family and Friends Influence Your Health," *University of Texas Lifetime Health Letter,* February 1995, 1, 8.

14. As cited in Gary Smalley and John Trent, *The Hidden Value of a Man: The Incredible Impact of a Man on His Family* (Colorado Springs: Focus on the Family, 1992), 136-37.

15. As cited in John R. O'Neil, *The Paradox of Success: When Winning at Work Means Losing at Life* (New York: G. P. Putnam's Sons, 1993), 111.

16. See for example, James Osterhaus, *Bonds of Iron: Forging Lasting Male Relationships* (Chicago: Moody Press, 1994).

17. See the pioneering work by Deborah Tannen, *You Just Don't Understand: Women and Men in Conversation* (New York: Morrow, 1990), which explores the different styles of communication between men and women.

18. Mike Corell, as quoted in Anita Sharpe, "How to Find Guys to Hang Around and Do Stuff With," *Wall Street Journal,* 9 May 1994, A-1.

19. As quoted in Judy Foreman, "It's True: Friends Can Save Your Life," *Denver Post,* 18 October 1992, 38A. For supportive evidence see "Stress and Immunity in Humans: Modifying Variables," by

Nicholas R. S. Hall, Julie A. Anderson and Maureen P. O'Grady, in *Handbook of Human Stress and Immunity*, ed. Ronald Glaser and Janice K. Kiecolt-Glaser (San Diego: Academic Press, 1994), 188-91.

20. Sheldon Cohen and others, "Chronic Social Stress, Affiliation, and Cellular Immune Response in Non Human Primates, *Psychological Science*, September 1992, 301-4.

21. "The Mind, The Body, and the Immune System: Part II," *Harvard Mental Health Letter*, 8 (February 1992): 3.

22. David Spiegel and others, "Effect of Psychosocial Treatment on Survival of Patients with Metastic Breast Cancer," *Lancet*, 14 October 1989, 888-91.

23. The research of University of Texas (El Paso) Professor Rey C. Martinez is reported in Russell Wild, "The ABCs of Men's Health," *Men's Health*, September 1995, 106.

24. Kent and Barbara Hughes, *Liberating Ministry from the Success Syndrome* (Wheaton, Ill.: Tyndale, 1991), 147-49. Second Corinthians 7:6 is as quoted on p. 147.

25. Michelle Ventor as quoted in *Acts of Faith*, ed. Ivanla Vanzant (New York: Fireside, 1993), meditation for July 15.

26. *Papyrus Oxyrhynchus* 840:2 as translated in John Dominic Crossan, ed. *Sayings Parallels: A Workbook for the Jesus Tradition* (Philadelphia: Fortress Press, 1986), 73.

27. As quoted by the *New York Times*, and picked up by Chuck Shepherd, "News of the Weird," *Charlottesville [Virginia] Weekly*, 28 March–3 April 1995.

28. Charles Misner, as quoted in *Origins: The Lives and Worlds of Modern Cosmologists*, ed. Alan Lightman and Roberta Brawer (Cambridge, Mass.: Harvard University Press, 1990), 247.

29. Richard Preston, "Crisis in the Hot Zone," *New Yorker*, 26 October 1992, 62.

30. Quoted in Timothy C. Morgan, "The War Against HIV," *Christianity Today*, 4 April 1994, 73.

31. This theme is developed more fully in Leonard I. Sweet and K. Elizabeth Rennie, "Waiting Rooms," *Homiletics*, October–December 1993, 43-46.

32. Charles Handy, *The Age of Paradox* (Boston: Harvard Business School Press, 1994), 21.

33. Thomas Moore, *Meditations: On the Monk Who Dwells in Daily Life* (New York: HarperCollins, 1994), 83.

34. Sarah Dunn, *The Official Slacker Handbook* (New York: Warner, 1994), 6.

35. The spark plug for this "voluntary simplicity" movement is the New Road Map Foundation, started by Joseph R. Dominguez and Vicki Robin, whose best-selling book *Your Money or Your Life: Transforming Your Relationship with Money and Achieving Financial Independence* (New York: Viking, 1992) is transforming the social landscape.

36. Randall Rothenberg, "What Makes Sammy Walk?" *Esquire,* May 1995, 72-79.
37. Juliet Schor, "Why (And How) More People Are Dropping Out of the Rat Race," *Working Woman,* August 1995, 14. I wish to thank Landrum Leavell III for this reference.
38. See the work of psychologists Dorothy and Jerome Singer, *The House of Make-Believe: Play and the Developing Imagination* (Cambridge, Mass.: Harvard University Press, 1990).
39. Ted Hughes, "Thrushes," *Faber Book of Modern Verse,* ed. Michael Roberts, 3d ed. (London: Faber & Faber, 1965), 398.

3. Play Out the Child in You

1. Stanley Kuntz, *Next-to-Last Things: New Poems and Essays* (New York: Atlantic Monthly Press, 1985), 119.
2. As quoted in Robert Wuthnow, *Christianity in the 21st Century* (New York: Oxford University Press, 1993), 195.
3. Wendell Berry, *Sex, Economy, Freedom & Community: Eight Essays* (New York: Pantheon Books, 1993), xiv.
4. "The U.S. Is Killing Its Young," *Utne Reader,* May/June 1994, 42.
5. Laurie Goodstein, "When Day Care and 'Traditional' Values Collide," *Washington Post Weekly* 11 (31 October 1994): 34.
6. As told by Jim Gorman in Ecunet [database online], cited 9 September 1994, meeting name: Bottom Drawer, filename A000000T.MSG.
7. Michel Quoist, *New Prayers,* trans. Elizabeth Lovatt-Dolan (New York: Crossroad, 1990), 165. Originally published as *Chemins de Prieres* (Paris: Les Editions Ouvrieres, 1988). English translation copyright Gill and Macmillan, 1989. Reprinted with permission of The Crossroad Publishing Company, New York.
8. Most notably, John Bradshaw in *Homecoming: Reclaiming and Championing Your Inner Child* (New York: Bantam, 1990).
9. Joseph A. Grassi, *The Secret Identity of the Beloved Disciple* (New York: Paulist Press, 1990), 115.
10. Ibid.
11. As quoted in Eric James, *Word Over All* (London: SPCK, 1992), 46.
12. John Dominic Crossan, ed. *Sayings Parallels: A Workbook for the Jesus Tradition* (Philadelphia: Fortress Press, 1986), 117.
13. In the *Gospel of Thomas* 21:1-2, there is this parable of the children in the field: "Mary said to Jesus, 'Whom are Your disciples like?' He said, 'They are like children who have settled in a field which is not theirs. When the owners of the field come, they will say, "Let us have back our field." They will undress in their presence in order to let them have back their field and to give it back to them.' " Crossan, *Sayings Parallels*, 20. Biblical scholar Larry Welborn was sharing his consternation over this parable with a class at United Theological

Seminary one day, when a student observed that nothing recalled the innocence and freedom of her childhood more forcefully than the memory of throwing off her clothes and dancing on them.

14. Michael McCoy, *The Child in Our Midst* (Johannesburg, South Africa: Department of Missionary Church of the Province of Southern Africa, 1987), 49.

15. Shunryu Suzuki, *Zen Mind, Beginner's Mind* (New York: Weatherhill, 1970), 21-22; or see this quote from Zen master Suzuki-roshi quoted in *The Tibetan Book of Living and Dying* by Sogyal Rinpoche (San Francisco: HarperSanFrancisco, 1992): "If your mind is empty, it is always ready for anything: it is open to everything. In the beginner's mind there are many possibilities, in the expert's mind there are few."

16. Andre Malraux, *Man's Fate (La Condition Humaine)* (New York: Harrison Smith and Robert Haas, 1934), 359-60.

17. George William Russell, "Germinal," *Collected Poems by A. E.* (London: Macmillan, 1935), 401.

18. Philip D. Schroeder, "From Illustration to Animation: Modeling a Paradigm Shift in Worship and Homiletics Through Children's Sermons" (D.Min. diss., United Theological Seminary, 1995), 40.

19. Brendan Kennelly, *Journey into Joy* (Newcastle upon Tyne, England: Bloodaxe, 1994).

20. Horace Bushnell, *Work and Play; or, Literary Varieties* (New York: Charles Scribner, 1864), 21-22.

21. Matthew 18:3, as creatively translated by Ronald Scales.

22. David Bohm and F. David Peat, *Science, Order, Creativity* (New York: Bantam, 1987), 48.

23. *The Life of Teresa of Jesus: The Autobiography of St. Teresa of Avila*, trans. and ed. E. Allison Peers (Garden City, N.Y.: Image Books, 1960), 145.

24. Roger von Oech, *A Whack on the Side of the Head: How to Unlock Your Mind for Innovation* (New York: Warner, 1983), 97.

25. Dorothy G. Singer and Jerome L. Singer, *The House of Make-Believe: Children's Play and the Developing Imagination* (Cambridge, Mass.: Harvard University Press, 1990), 199-229.

26. Rubem Azevedo Alves, "Play or How to Subvert the Dominant Values," *Union Seminary Quarterly Review* 26 (1970): 49.

27. See W. Andrew Ford, *Composer to Composer* (London: Allen & Unwin, 1994), 36.

28. W. Robert McClelland, *Worldly Spirituality* (St. Louis: CBP Press, 1990), 56.

29. Nikos Kazantzakis, *Report to Greco* (New York: Simon & Schuster, 1965).

4. Walk a Daily Dose of LSD (Long, Slow Distances)

1. "But even if I don't want to, it is still something that God has sent me to do" (1 Cor. 9:17 CEV).

2. Contrast this to Paul's references to pommeling his body to receive the prize (1 Cor. 9:24, 27), and "straining forward to what lies ahead" (Phil. 3:13) [for other allusions to sports see 1 Thess. 2:19; Gal. 2:2; Phil. 4:1; Col. 2:18; Eph. 6:12].

3. For the distinction between "sport," "sports," "physical education," and "play" see Robert J. Higgs, *Sports: A Reference Guide* (Westport, Conn.: Greenwood Press, 1982), 6.

4. Chrysostom, *Homily 57.*

5. In the words of *Health* magazine, as found in the Walking Health Information Card Supplement to *Health* (P.O. Box 56863, Boulder, CO 80322-6863).

6. For perceptions of the hazards of smoking, such as a 10.8 times greater chance of dying from lung cancer than nonsmokers, or a 6.1 times greater chance of dying of bronchitis or emphysema, and so forth, see W. Kip Viscusi's *Smoking: Making the Risky Decision* (New York: Oxford University Press, 1993).

7. *University of Texas Lifetime Health Letter,* September 1994, 6.

8. As reported in "Heart Beat," *University of Texas Lifetime Health Letter,* October 1994, 6.

9. Covert Bailey, *Smart Exercise: Burning Fat, Getting Fit* (Boston: Houghton Mifflin, 1994).

10. For an easy-to-use method of designing your own walking program, send a self-addressed, 55-cent stamped envelope to Rockport Walking Test, c/o The Rockport Walking Institute, 72 Howe Street, Marlboro, MA 01752. To join any number of walking clubs, write the National Organization of Mall Walkers, P.O. Box 191, Hermann, MO 65041.

11. See the study reported in the *Journal of the American Geriatrics Society,* as reported in *University of Texas Lifetime Health Letter,* May 1994, 2.

12. A daily half-hour stroll has been shown to increase scores on intelligence tests. See Joannie M. Schrof, "Brain Power," *U.S. News & World Report,* 28 November 1994, 94.

13. Joan Puls, *Seek Treasures in Small Fields* (Mystic, Conn.: Twenty-Third Publications, 1993), 38.

14. Larry Laudan, *The Book of Risks* (New York: John Wiley & Sons, 1994), 45, 56.

15. Lyle Schaller, *The Seven-Day-a-Week Church* (Nashville: Abingdon Press, 1992), 163.

16. Quoted in "NB" column, *TLS: Times Literary Supplement,* 4 February 1994, 14.

17. Henry Miller, *The Complete Book of Friends* (London: Allison & Busby, 1988), 209-14.

18. Ed Ayres, "Breaking Away," *World Watch,* January/February 1992. Ayres shows how "Each year, cars kill more children, women, and men in accidents than most armies lose in wars; they imprison millions of people for two to three hours a day; contribute to epi-

demic levels of lung and heart disease; and threaten the stability of the climate itself" (11).

19. U.S. census data, 1990.

20. A 1993 U.S. Bureau of the Census report finds that less than 1 percent of Americans ride bicycles to work, while 88 percent commute by car.

21. *New York Times,* 9 December 1994, 16.

22. Jan Larson, "The Bicycle Market," *American Demographics,* March 1995, 42-50.

23. As reported in *John Naisbitt's Trend Letter,* 30 March 1995, 8.

24. Marcia D. Lowe, "Bicycle Production Rises Again," *World Watch,* September/October 1994, 38.

25. Kevin W. Wildes, "In the Name of the Father," *New Republic,* 26 December 1994, 21-25.

26. For Lovett Weems's application of Peters's principles to the church, see *Church Leadership: Vision, Team, Culture and Integrity* (Nashville: Abingdon Press, 1993), 53.

27. Used by permission, with my thanks to Max Williams.

28. As quoted in "NB" column, *TLS,* 26 March 1993, 14.

29. Walker Percy, *Sign-Posts in a Strange Land* (New York: Farrar, Straus & Giroux, 1991), 302.

30. Personal conversation with Bernard Brandon Scott.

31. Jim Corbett, *Goatwalking* (New York: Viking, 1991), 4.

32. See Leonard I. Sweet and K. Elizabeth Rennie, "Goatwalking to Bethlehem," *Homiletics,* October-December 1993, 39-42.

33. Steve Hawthorn and Graham Kendrick, *PrayerWalking* (London: Kingsway, 1990); see also Leonard I. Sweet and K. Elizabeth Rennie, "Prayer-Walking," *Homiletics,* (October-December 1994), 23-26.

34. As quoted in Robert Winterhalter with George W. Fisk, *Jesus' Parables: Finding Our God Within* (New York: Paulist Press, 1993), 58.

35. As quoted in Lonnie Collins Pratt, "Why Pray When You Don't See Answers," *Discipleship Journal,* January/February 1994, 78.

36. Thomas Keating, *Intimacy with God* (New York: Crossroad, 1994), 115.

37. As told in Ysenda Maxtone Graham, *The Church Hesitant: A Portrait of the Church of England Today* (London: Hodder & Stoughton, 1993), 207.

5. Mind Your Thoughts

1. See Julius Wellhausen, *Einleitung in die drei ersten Evangelien* (Berlin: Georg Reimer, 1905). With thanks to Dr. Larry Welborn for the translation.

2. According to the *Gospel of Thomas* 89, "Jesus said, Why do you wash the outside of the cup? Do you not understand that the one who made the inside is also the one who made the outside?" *The*

Gospel of Thomas: The Hidden Sayings of Jesus, trans. Marvin Meyer (San Francisco: HarperSanFrancisco, 1992), 59.

3. F. F. Centore, *Persons: A Comparative Account of the Six Possible Theories* (Westport, Conn.: Greenwood Press, 1979). The other categories are reductionist materialism, nonreductionist materialism, first-order psychosomaticism, vitalism, and reductionist immaterialism.

4. Moshe Mykoff, *The Empty Chair: Finding Hope and Joy: Timeless Wisdom from a Hasidic Master, Rebbe Nachman of Breslov* (Woodstock, Vt.: Jewish Lights Publishing, 1994), 20.

5. Christine Gorman, "Why, You Don't Look a Day Over 100!" *Time*, Special Issue "Beyond the Year 2000: What to Expect in the New Millennium," fall 1992, 55.

6. So warns Stanford University psychiatrist David Spiegel in "Psychosocial Intervention in Cancer," *Journal of the National Cancer Institute* 85 (4 August 1993): 1198. Also see his book *Living Beyond Limits* (New York: Times Books, 1993).

7. See the 1993 PBS special "Healing and the Mind with Bill Moyers," available on videocassette as *Healing and the Mind*, by Bill Moyers (New York: David Gruber Productions, 1993).

8. See Peter Steinfels, "Psychiatrists' Manual Shifts Stance on Religious and Spiritual Problems," *New York Times* 10 February 1994, A16.

9. *Mind, Body Medicine: How to Use Your Mind for Better Health*, ed. Daniel Goelman and Joel Gurin (Yonkers, N.Y.: Consumer Reports Books, 1993). Also see the abbreviated version "Can Your Mind Heal Your Body?" *Consumer Reports* 58 (February 1993): 107-15.

10. Indeed, it is the human category to think, not God's. The theologians' aspiration to "think God's thoughts after Him" fails to comprehend that God is not generated by thought. God doesn't possess thoughts, nor does God "think." God *is* thought. God doesn't possess powers or love. God *is* power. God is love.

11. See Delia Cioffi and James Holloway, "Delayed Costs of Suppressed Pain," *Journal of Personality and Social Psychology* 64 (February 1993): 274-82.

12. Blair Justice hammers this theme home in his *Who Gets Sick? How Beliefs, Moods, and Thoughts Affect Your Health* (Los Angeles: Jeremy Tarcher, 1988).

13. While Anthony Thiselton and Robert Carroll would have us think of this kind of language as performative, there are many (like Harold Bloom) who are drawn to Giambattista Vico's view of the origin of language, with Walter Benjamin even viewing language "magically." See W. Menninghaus, *Walter Benjamin's Theorie der Sprachmagic* (Frankfurt am Mainz: Suhrkamp Verlag, 1980).

14. Carl Sagan, "Scam or Miracle?" *Parade Magazine*, 4 December 1994, 9.

15. John Locke, *Essay Concerning Human Understanding*, 2.10.5, in *The Works of John Locke* (London: Printed for W. Otridge and Son, 1812), 1:130-31.

16. Jonathan Edwards, *Treatise on Religious Affections,* abridged by John Wesley, in Wesley's *A Christian Library* (London: J. Kershaw, 1827), 30:321.
17. This notion has given rise to Catharine MacKinnon's argument that pornography itself is rape because saying can be doing, and speech or pictures can themselves be violence. See Catharine MacKinnon, *Only Words* (Cambridge, Mass.: Harvard University Press, 1993), 29.
18. Buck Anderson, "Rediscovering the Lost Art of Meditation," *Kindred Spirit* 18 (winter 1994): 10-12.
19. Michael Marriott, "Living in 'Lockdown'," *Newsweek,* 23 January 1995, 56-57.
20. V. A. C. Gatreel, *The Hanging Tree: Execution and the English People, 1770-1868* (London: Oxford University Press, 1994).
21. As quoted in *Current Thoughts & Trends,* March 1995, 13.
22. Michael Medved, "Pop Culture and Your Kids," *Lutheran Witness* 113 (May 1994): 3-6.
23. Carl M. Cannon, "Honey, I Warped the Kids," *Mother Jones,* July/August 1993, 16-17.
24. Paul Farhi, "TV Violence Adds Punch to the Overseas Market," *Washington Post Weekly,* 13 February 1995, 21.
25. L. Rowell Huesmann, "Cross-National Commonalities in the Learning of Aggression from Media Violence," in *Television and the Aggressive Child: A Cross-National Comparison,* ed. Huesmann and Leonard D. Eron (Hillsdale, N.J.: Erlbaum Associates, 1986), 244, as quoted in Dorothy G. Singer and Jerome L. Singer, *The House of Make-Believe: Children's Play and the Developing Imagination* (Cambridge, Mass.: Harvard University Press, 1990), 257.
26. Betsy McAlister Groves and others, "Silent Victims: Children Who Witness Violence," *JAMA: Journal of the American Medical Society* 269 (13 January 1993): 262.
27. Brandon S. Centerwall, "Television and Violence," *JAMA:* 267 (10 June 1992): 3061.
28. Brandon S. Centerwall, "Exposure to Television as a Risk Factor for Violence," *American Journal of Epidemiology* 129 (1989): 643-52.
29. Centerwall, "Television and Violence," 3059.
30. Ibid., 3062.
31. Ibid., 3059.
32. Senators Ernest Hollings and Daniel Inouye are cosponsoring a bill to ban any act of violence on television before a specified time (midnight, for example).
33. John Dominic Crossan, *Sayings Parallels: A Workbook for the Jesus Tradition* (Philadelphia: Fortress Press, 1986), 37.
34. See "The Mind-Body Connection: Emotions and Disease," *University of Texas Lifetime Health Letter,* February 1994, 1, 6, 8.

35. See this saying on "Knowing Oneself" from the *Gospel of Thomas* 3, "When you know yourselves, then you will be known, and you will understand that you are children of the living father. But if you do not know yourselves, then you dwell in poverty, and you are poverty." See *Gospel of Thomas,* trans. Harold Bloom, 23.
36. David B. Morris, *The Culture of Pain* (Berkeley: University of California Press, 1991), 29-30, 75-76.
37. See Mark Matousek, "Savage Grace," *Common Boundary,* May/June 1993, 22-31.
38. So argues Cornell University psychologist Alice M. Isen.
39. As referenced in Robert Ornstein and David Sobel, *The Healing Brain* (New York: Simon & Schuster, 1987), 159-60.
40. See Allan Luks and Peggy Payne's well-researched *The Healing Power of Doing Good: The Health and Spiritual Benefits of Helping Others* (New York: Fawcett Columbine, 1992), which documents the health improvements among AIDS patients and others involved in volunteerism.
41. See also the work of psychologist Harville Hendrix for the inability of the "old brain" to distinguish giving to others and giving to oneself (i.e., *Getting the Love You Want* [New York: HarperCollins], 1990, and *Keeping the Love You Find* [New York Pocket Books], 1992).
42. The best definition of PS^2 is found in Neil Solomon's *Sick & Tired of Being Sick & Tired* (New York: Wynwood Press, 1989): "a hyper-reactivity of the body to any stressor, or sensitizer, that results in illness that may not seem at first glance to have a clear-cut medical cause" (37-38).
43. In the world of PNI, an immunological overreaction is called allergy; conversely, an immunological underreaction is called AIDS.
44. Redford B. Williams and Virginia Williams, *Anger Kills: Seventeen Strategies for Controlling the Hostility That Can Harm Your Health* (New York: Random House, 1993), xiii.
45. Quoted in James and Evelyn Whitehead, *Shadows of the Heart* (New York: Crossroad, 1994), 13.
46. This study, which was reported in the *American Journal of Cardiology,* was summarized in *University of Texas Lifetime Health Letter,* November 1992, 5.
47. Fred McCarthy, "Telltale Heart," *Omni,* March 1994, 30.
48. Renaissance artists celebrated the sexuality of Jesus in ways that embarrass us today (nude body, ordinary genitals, often in a state of erection)—leading our immediate forebears, for example, to paint diapers on cherubs and infants.
49. A special thanks to Daile Boulis for insisting that I not omit God's acceptance of anger and grief.
50. As quoted in "Sunbeams," *The Sun,* February 1994, 40.
51. See Williams and Williams, *Anger Kills.*
52. As reported in "Taking Hopeless to Heart," *Science News,* 31 July 1993, 79.

53. Marvin Stein, Andrew H. Miller, and Robert L. Trestman, "Depression: the Immune System, and Health and Illness," *Archives of General Psychiatry* 48 (February 1991): 171-77; Andrew H. Miller, ed., *Depressive Disorders and Immunity* (Washington D.C.: American Psychiatric Press, 1989).

54. "The Mind, the Body, and the Immune System: Part II," *The Harvard Mental Health Letter* 8 (February 1992): 3.

55. Erwin Schrödinger, *What Is Life? The Physical Aspect of the Living Cell and Mind and Matter* (London: Cambridge University Press, 1969), 145.

56. K.A. Fackelmann and J. Raloff, "Psychological Stress Linked to Cancer," *Science News*, 25 September 1993, 196.

57. The closing exhortation from a 1995 sermon entitled "The Spiritual Renewal of America" as given in Breyfogel Chapel, United Theological Seminary, Dayton, Ohio.

58. "Associations Between Dimensions of Religious Commitment and Mental Health Reported in the *American Journal of Psychiatry and Archives of General Psychiatry*, 1978-1989," *American Journal of Psychiatry* 149 (April 1992): 557-59.

59. As reported in *National & International Religion Report* 6 (2 November 1992): 4.

60. See Arthur A. Stone, Laura S. Porter, and John M. Neale, "Daily Events and Mood Prior to the Onset of Respiratory Illness Episodes: A Non-replication of the 3-5 Day 'Desirability Dip,' *British Journal of Medical Psychology* 66 (1993), 383-93.

61. Joachim Jeremias, *The Eucharistic Words of Jesus* (Philadelphia: Fortress Press, 1977), 54-55.

62. Deryck Cooke, *The Language of Music* (London: Oxford University Press, 1959).

63. See *Music and Miracles*, comp. Don Campbell (Wheaton, Ill.: Quest Books, 1992).

64. Solomon, *Sick & Tired of Being Sick & Tired*, 92.

65. As quoted in Karen Granberg-Michaelson, *Healing Community* (Geneva: WCC Publications, 1991), 7.

66. Bernie S. Siegel, *Love, Medicine, and Miracles: Lessons Learned About Self-Healing from a Surgeon's Experience with Exceptional Patients* (New York: Harper & Row, 1986), 181.

67. As quoted by Eric R. Ram in *Health, Healing and Transformation: Biblical Reflections on the Church in Ministries of Healing & Wholeness* (Monrovia, Calif.: World Vision International, 1991), 103.

68. See Michael Talbot, *The Holographic Universe* (New York: HarperCollins, 1991), 51.

69. *The Holy Scriptures According to the Masoretic Text* (Philadelphia: Jewish Publication Society of America, 1942).

70. As quoted in Morris Maddocks, *The Healing Ministry*, 2nd ed. (London: SPCK, 1990), 234.

71. I love this version in Ignatius: "Unless a man be within the sanctu-

ary, he lacks the bread of God, for if prayer of one or two has such might, how much more has that . . . of the whole Church? "Ignatius to the Ephesians," *The Epistles of Saint Ignatius,* in *The Apostolic Fathers,* trans. Kirsopp Lake (Cambridge, Mass.: Harvard University Press, 1949) 2:179.

6. Set the Table

1. This is the thesis of Gillian Feeley-Harnik, *The Lord's Table: The Meaning of Food in Early Judaism and Christianity* (Washington, D.C.: Smithsonian Press, 1994).
2. See John Dominic Crossan, ed., *Jesus: A Revolutionary Biography* (San Francisco: HarperSanFrancisco, 1994).
3. This phrase, "Jesus ate good food with bad people" is not mine. I have heard it from so many sources, however, that I am not able to authenticate its attribution.
4. See also Luke 10:7; 10:38-42; 11:37-44; 13:29; 14:1-6; 14:7-14; 14:15-24; 15:23; 16:19-31; 19:5-10.
5. See also Acts 4:32-35; 9:19; 10:9-16; 10:23; 10:48; 11:3; 10:48; 11:3; 16:34; 20:7, 11; 27:33-38.
6. J. Duncan M. Derrett, "Jesus's Fishermen and the Parable of the Net," *Novum Testamentum* 22 (1980): 133.
7. Otto Betz, "Was John the Baptist an Essene?" in *Understanding the Dead Sea Scrolls: A Reader from the Biblical Archaeology Review,* ed. Hershel Shanks (New York: Random House, 1992), 205-14.
8. Dennis E. Smith, "The Historical Jesus at Table," *Society of Biblical Literature 1989 Seminar Papers,* ed. David J. Lull (Atlanta: Scholars Press, 1989), 467. Smith ends his article, however, with this conclusion: "What is being identified as the historical Jesus at table is more likely to be the idealized characterization of Jesus at table that is produced in the early Christian community. The social realities of such meals are still being correctly assessed, but the one who presents parabolic messages by means of meal practices is more likely to be the idealized Jesus rather than the historical Jesus" (486). I would argue, in contrast, that the historical figure of Jesus was consonant, not dissonant, with these traditions of the early Christian community.
9. Former president of the Southern Baptist Convention, who has lost a daughter-in-law and a grandson to AIDS, and who has another grandson who is HIV-positive. Allen also has a gay son with AIDS. As quoted in Martin E. Marty's *Context,* 15 November 1994, 6.
10. Norman Perrin, *Rediscovering the Teaching of Jesus* (New York: Harper & Row, 1967), 102-8.
11. Peter Farb and George Armelagos, *Consuming Passions: The Anthropology of Eating* (Boston: Houghton Mifflin, 1980), 4, 211; as quoted by John Dominic Crossan, *Jesus, A Revolutionary Biography* (San Francisco: HarperSanFrancisco, 1994), 68.

12. Feeley-Harnik, *The Lord's Table*, 72.
13. This continues the argument of Feeley-Harnik, *The Lord's Table*.
14. Mary Louise Bringle, "Swallowing the Shame: Pastoral Care Issues in Food Abuse," *Journal of Pastoral Care* 48 (summer 1994): 135-44; see also Bringle *The God of Thinness: Gluttony and Other Weighty Matters* (Nashville: Abingdon Press, 1992).
15. This statistic is revealed in "Losing Weight: The Truth Is Hard to Swallow," *Health Letter* 10 (April 1994): 1.
16. June Cotner, *Graces: Prayers and Poems for Everyday Meals and Special Occasions* (San Francisco: HarperSanFrancisco, 1994), 7.
17. J. Raloff, "Diet Changes May Buy Cancer Patients Time," *Science News*, 14 November 1992, 324.
18. For arguments that Jesus was a vegetarian, see Rynn Berry, *Famous Vegetarians and Their Favourite Recipes: Lives and Lore from Buddha to Beatles* (Los Angeles: Panjandrum Books, 1989), 21-27; for arguments that he was not, see Roger T. Beckwith, "The Vegetarianism of the Therapeutae, and the Motives for Vegetarianism in Early Jewish and Christian Circles," *Revue de Qumran* 13 (1988): 407-10.
19. See chapter 10 "The Religious Basis for Vegetarianism" in Lewis G. Regenstein, *Replenish the Earth: A History of Organized Religion's Treatment of Animals and Nature—Including the Bible's Message of Conservation and Kindness Toward Animals* (New York: Crossroad, 1991), 176-77.
20. As quoted in Joan Franks, "One Woman's View from 40," *Utne Reader*, January/February 1990, 84.
21. Compare Isa. 65:25. For information on John Wesley, see *Sermons on Several Occasions* (New York: J. Soule and T. Mason, 1818), 2:113, 167-69.
22. For condemnations of meat-eating in the prophetic books, Psalms and Proverbs, see Amos 6:4; Isa. 7:21-22; 22:13-14; Ezek. 47:12; Jer. 7:16, 21; 16:13, 19; Joel 2:19; Ps. 5:6-10; 50:9-10, 13; Prov. 23:20-21.
23. See Jeremy Rifkin's *Beyond Beef: The Rise and Fall of the Cattle Culture* (New York: Dutton, 1992).
24. Marc Reisner and Sarah Bates, *Overtapped Oasis: Reform or Revolution for Western Water* (Washington, D.C.: Island Press, 1990), 32-33.
25. Francis X. Clooney, "Vegetarianism and Religion," *America*, 24 February 1979, 133.
26. There were 48.3 million tons of grain fed to beef cattle in 1973–74. UNICEF and the Food and Agriculture Organization at the United Nations estimate that ten million tons of grain are needed to ward off starvation. Two fewer weeks in a feed lot, which would hardly affect the taste of the beef, would save ten million tons of grain. See Stanley C. Baldwin, "A Case Against Waste and Other Excesses," *Christianity Today*, 16 July 1976, 1066, 1068.
27. For the Seeds of Change philosophy, as outlined by founder Gabriel Howearth, write for a catalog to 621 Old Santa Fe Trail, No. 10, Santa Fe, NM 87501.

28. Paul Theroux, *Millroy the Magician* (New York: Random House, 1994), 28.
29. Ibid., 216.
30. Ann Misch, "Richer Diets Risk Breast Cancer," *WorldWatch*, November/December 1992, 35-36.
31. "Keeping Cancer at Bay with Diet," *Johns Hopkins Medical Letter: Health after 50* 6 (April 1994): 1.
32. K. A. Fackelmann, "Dietary Fat Predicts Breast Cancer's Course," *Science News*, 9 January 1993, 23.
33. See "Andrew Linzey Replies," *Christian Century* 11 December 1991, 1181. This and other "Locating Animals in God's Realm," reader responses by H. A. Lueking, Jr., David Feddes, Paul J. Westcott, Dennis Myhand, and Karl E. Buff in the 11 December issue (1179-82) are in response to Linzey's "The Theological Basis of Animal Rights," *Christian Century*, 9 October 1991, 906-9.
34. Paul Beckett, "Eat Pounds of Meat, Drink Gallons of Ale and Be a Very Merry Monk," *Wall Street Journal*, 23 November 1994, B1.
35. William H. Drummond, *The Rights of Animals and Man's Obligation to Treat Them with Humanity* (London: J. Mardon, 1838), 30-31.
36. Jim Corbett, *Goatwalking* (New York: Viking, 1991), 44.
37. See Bob Schwartz, *Diets Don't Work* (Galveston, Tex.: Breakthru Pub., 1982), 151-68.
38. Paul and Linda McCartney, "If It Has a Face Don't Eat It!" in *The Way Ahead: A Visionary Perspective for the New Millennium*, ed. Eddie and Bobbie Shapiro (Rockport, Mass.: Element, 1992), 133.
39. See Stuart Berger, *Dr. Berger's Immune Power Diet* (New York: New American Library, 1985); Berger, *Forever Young: 20 Years Younger in 20 Weeks: Dr. Berger's Step-by-Step Rejuvenating Program* (New York: Morrow, 1989); and Berger, *How to Be Your Own Nutritionist* (New York: Morrow, 1987).

7. Adopt a See-You-at-the-Party Spirit

1. For one source of this translation, see the work of the lay theologian John Scotus Erigena, whom some have seen as "the only philosophical alternative in the West to the Aristotelian scholasticism of St. Thomas Aquinas," in *The Voice of the Eagle: Homily on the Prologue to the Gospel of St. John*, trans. with an introduction and reflections by Christopher Bamford (Hudson, N.Y.: Lindisfarne Press, 1990), 33.
2. As quoted in C. S. Lewis, *George MacDonald: An Anthology* (London: Geoffrey Bles, The Centenary Press, 1946), 19.
3. Sheldon Vanauken, *A Severe Mercy* (San Francisco: Harper & Row, 1977), 189.
4. For a fuller development of Ignazio Silone's thought, see *The Story of a Humble Christian* (New York: Harper & Row, 1968), 16, 30-32.

5. See Robert N. Bellah and others, *The Good Society* (New York: Knopf, 1991), 206.
6. This is the answer to the first question of the Westminster Catechism. See for example, Alexander Whyte, *A Commentary on the Shorter Catechism* (Edinburgh: T. & T. Clark, n.d.), 1.
7. Augustine's complete statement reads: "I would state firmly: You are only partly drawn by your will. You are more drawn by total pleasure."
8. Herman Arndt, *Why Did Jesus Fast?* (Cincinnati: Printed for the Author, 1922), 9.
9. John Dominic Crossan, ed. *Sayings Parallels: A Workbook for the Jesus Tradition* (Philadelphia: Fortress Press, 1986), 119.
10. Abel Stevens, *History of the Methodist Episcopal Church in the United States of America* (New York: Nelson & Phillips, 1864), 2:134.
11. See Tertullian, "*De Jejuniis.*" For English trans. see "On Fasting: On Opposition to the Psychics," in *The Ante-Nicene Fathers: Translations of the Writings of the Fathers Down to A.D. 325*, ed. Alexander Roberts and James Donaldson (Grand Rapids, Mich.: Eerdmans 1972), 4:102-14.
12. See Mark 9:29, although some manuscripts omit "and fasting." See note in the NRSV.
13. John Piper, *Desiring God* (Portland, Ore.: Multnomah Press, 1986).
14. Robert Farrar Capon, *An Offering of Uncles: The Priesthood of Adam and the Shape of the World* (New York: Sheed and Ward, 1967), 90.
15. H. L. Mencken, *Minority Report: H. L. Mencken's Notebooks* (New York: Knopf, 1956), 214.
16. As quoted in Jonathon Green's *The Cynic's Lexicon* (New York: St. Martin's Press, 1984), 47.
17. A. De la Peña, *The Psychobiology of Cancer* (Westport, Conn.: Greenwood Press, 1983).
18. A. J. P. Taylor, *Letters to Eva: 1969–1983*, ed. Eva Haraszti Taylor (London: Century, 1991), 12.
19. As cited in Piper, *Desiring God*, 203.
20. See Robert Williams, *Just As I Am: A Practical Guide to Being Out, Proud, and Christian* (New York: Crown Publishers, 1992). Williams is sometimes called, albeit mistakenly, the first openly gay man to be ordained in the Episcopal Church.
21. Raymond E. Brown, *New Testament Essays* (Milwaukee: Bruce Pub. Co., 1965), 167.
22. David Lowes Watson's words, spoken in the presence of the author.
23. Elizabeth Barnes, *The Story of Discipleship* (Nashville: Abingdon Press, 1995), 60.
24. Ibid., 67-68.
25. John Dominic Crossan, *Jesus, A Revolutionary Biography* (San Francisco: HarperSanFrancisco, 1994), 54.
26. See *Nag Hammadi Codex III, 5: The Dialogue of the Savior*, Stephen Emmel, ed. (Leiden, Netherlands: Brill, 1984), 83.
27. Michael Curtin, *The Plastic Tomato Cutter* (London: Abacus, 1993), 12.

28. Translation of the Epigraph to Graham Greene's *The Heart of the Matter* (New York: Viking, 1948). It appears as "Le pécheur est au couer même de chrétienté. . . . Nul n'est aussi competent que le pécheur en matière de chrétienté. Nul, si ce n'est le saint."

29. Joseph Grassi, *The Secret Identity of the Beloved Disciple* (New York: Paulist Press, 1990), 88-90.

30. E. P. Sanders, *Jesus and Judaism* (Philadelphia: Fortress Press, 1986), 177. See also Sanders' contention that Jesus "may have offered their [i.e., sinners'] inclusion in the kingdom not only *while they were sinners* but also *without* requiring repentance, as normally understood, and therefore he could have been accused of being a friend of people who indefinitely *remained* sinners" (206; cf. 207-8).

31. Emma J. and Ludwig Edelstein, *Asclepius: A Collection and Interpretation of the Testimonies* (Baltimore: Johns Hopkins Press, 1945), 2:175.

32. Edgar Hennecke, *New Testament Apocrypha*, ed. Wilhelm Schneemelcher, trans. R. McL. Wilson (Philadelphia: Westminster Press, 1963), 1:148.

33. Jane Schaberg, *The Illegitimacy of Jesus: A Feminist Theological Interpretation of the Infancy Narratives* (San Francisco: Harper & Row, 1987).

8. Come Apart So You Don't Come Apart

1. For Freud's psychoneurosis, see the last chapter "The Therapeutic God," in Roy Porter, *A Social History of Madness: The World Through the Eyes of the Insane* (New York: Weidenfeld and Nicolson, 1987), 214.

2. For an excellent analysis of how surroundings may shape one's thought, emotion, and action, see Winifred Gallagher, *The Power of Place: How Our Surroundings Shape Our Thoughts, Emotions, and Actions* (New York: Poseidon Press, 1993).

3. John Dominic Crossan, ed. *Sayings Parallels: A Workbook for the Jesus Tradition* (Philadelphia: Fortress Press, 1986), 123.

4. See James Breech, *The Silence of Jesus: The Authentic Voice of the Historical Man* (Philadelphia: Fortress Press, 1983).

5. Thich Nhat Hanh, *Touching Peace: Practicing the Art of Mindful Living* (Berkeley, Calif.: Parallax Press, 1992), 1.

6. In the medieval era people esteemed the "book of creation" or what they called "the book of nature" a sacred text. See also eighteenth-century advocates of "the book of nature" like St. Therese of Lisieux, or Nicodemos of the Holy Mountain, an Orthodox writer who writes "In fact, there is a great symphony and unity between these two, so that nature is an explanation of scripture and scripture of nature." As quoted in Charles Cummings, *Eco-Spirituality: Toward a Reverent Life* (New York: Paulist Press, 1991), 43.

7. Nancy Marx Better, "Separating the Fugitives from the Stress Fighters," *New York Times*, 25 August 1991, Sec. 3, 25.

8. Jean Shinoda Bolen, *Crossing to Avalon* (San Francisco: HarperSanFrancisco, 1994), 28.

9. William A. Quayle, *Out-of-Doors with Jesus* (New York: Abingdon Press, 1924), 9.

10. Wendell Berry, *Sex, Economy, Freedom & Community* (New York: Pantheon, 1993), 103.

11. William George Roll, "Memory and the Long Body" in *Research in Parapsychology 1988*, ed. L. Henkel and R. Burger (Metuchen, N.J.: Scarecrow Press, 1989), 68.

12. Geoffrey R. Lilburne, *A Sense of Place: A Christian Theology of the Land* (Nashville: Abingdon Press, 1989), 96.

13. Stephen D. Moore, *Mark and Luke in Poststructuralist Perspectives: Jesus Begins to Write* (New Haven: Yale University Press, 1992), 24.

14. At his baptism Jesus saw the Spirit of God descending like a dove (Matt. 3:16; Mark 1:10; John saw it in John 1:32) or "in bodily form of a dove" (Luke 3:21).

15. John A. Sanford, *Mystical Christianity* (New York: Crossroad, 1993), 244.

16. Nigel Rees, *Epitaphs: A Dictionary of Grave Epigrams and Memorial Eloquence* (New York: Carroll & Graf Publications, 1993), 240.

17. Jesus called the Pharisees and Sadducees a "brood of vipers" (Matt. 3:7); see also Matt. 12:34; Matt. 23:33; and John the Baptist called the crowds that came to him for baptism, "You brood of vipers" (Luke 3:7).

18. Gore Vidal, *Live from Golgotha* (New York: Random House, 1992), 118.

19. See Richard Sorabji, *Animal Minds and Human Morals: The Origins of the Western Debate* (Ithaca, N.Y.: Cornell University Press, 1994).

20. See Mary Lee Daughtery, "Serpent-Handling as Sacrament," *Theology Today*, 232-42.

21. As quoted in "A Friend Indeed," *Harvard Health Letter*, 19 (December 1993): 1-3.

22. Judith M. Siegel, "Stressful Life Events and Use of Physician Services Among the Elderly: The Moderating Role of Pet Ownership," *Journal of Personality and Social Psychology* 58 (June 1990): 1081-86. See also Siegel, "Companion Animals: In Sickness and in Health," *Journal of Social Issues* 49 (spring 1993): 157-67.

23. For information on The Delta Society call 206-226-7357 or write P.O. Box 1080, Renton, WA 98057-9906. PAWS (Pets Are Wonderful Support) offers information and help to people with AIDS. Call 415-241-1460 or write 539 Castro Street, San Francisco, CA 94114.

24. *Dayton Daily News*, 13 November 1994, CALVIN AND HOBBES © Watterson. Reprinted with permission of UNIVERSAL PRESS SYNDICATE. All rights reserved.

25. David Attenborough, *Life on Earth: Natural History* (Boston: Little, Brown and Company, 1979), 20.

26. Jürgen Moltmann, "Christ in Cosmic Context," in *Christ and Context*, ed. Hilary Regan and Alan J. Torrance (Edinburgh: T. & T. Clark, 1993), 180-91.

27. John 12:32. The Greek word that is often translated as "every man" or "all people" is *pantas* or *pas*, which actually means "all things," or "every way."

28. Fred Krueger, "Why Ecology Is a Christian Issue," *Green Cross*, winter 1995, 16-17.

29. As quoted in *Common Boundary*, March/April 1995, 41.

30. Robert Ornstein and Paul Ehrlich point this out in their *New World, New Mind: Moving Through Conscious Evolution* (New York: Doubleday, 1989).

31. There is a helpful new version of this saying in the *Gospel of Thomas* 91: "You read the face of the sky and of the earth, but you have not recognized the one who . . . is before you, and you do not know how to read this moment." See Crossan, *Sayings Parallels*, 145.

32. From John Montague, "A Severed Head," pt. iv of *The Rough Field* (Dublin: Dolmen Press, 1972), 30.

33. Thanks to Professor Larry Welborn for this literal translation of Romans 1:18*b*.

34. See the 10 August 1992 fund-raising letter from Jacques-Yves Cousteau to The Cousteau Council, p. 3.

35. Paul Hawken, "The Ecology of Commerce," *Resurgence*, March/April 1993, 12.

36. Want to identify your unique type of forehead mites? Edward O. Wilson tells you how: "stretch the skin tight with one hand, carefully scrape a spatula or butter knife over the skin in the opposite direction, squeezing out traces of oily material from the sebum glands. (Avoid using too sharp an object, such as a glass edge or sharpened knife.) Next scrape the extracted material off the spatula with a cover slip and lower the slip face down onto a drop of immersion oil previously placed on a glass microscope slide. Then examine the material with an ordinary compound microscope. You will see the creatures that literally make your skin crawl." Edward O. Wilson's *The Diversity of Life* (Cambridge, Mass.: Belknap Press, 1992), 177-78.

37. Sigmund Kvaløy, "Inside Nature," *Resurgence*, November/ December 1992, 10.

38. See echoes of this in Albert J. LaChance's *Embracing Earth: Catholic Approaches to Ecology* (Maryknoll, N.Y.: Orbis Books, 1994).

39. Gerard Manley Hopkins, "Inversnaid," *The Book of Catholic Quotations*, sel. and ed. John Chapin (New York: Farrar, Straus and Cudahy, 1956), 913.

40. See *Hutchings' California Magazine*, as quoted in Simon Schama, "God's First Temples," *Times Literary Supplement: TLS*, 10 March 1995, 16.

9. Embrace the Unknown

1. See Gerard Hughes, *God of Surprises* (Boston: Cowley Publications, 1993).

2. The phrase is that of Bernard P. Prusak in "'The Son of Man Came Eating and Drinking': An Overview of Christological Perspectives on the Incarnation," *Who Do People Say I Am?* ed. Francis A. Eigo (Villanova, Pa.: Villanova University Press, 1980), 32-35.

3. Annie Dillard, "Seeing," in *Pilgrim at Tinker Creek* (New York: Harper's Magazine Press, 1974), 14-15.

4. T. S. Eliot, "Dry Salvages," *Four Quartets,* in Eliot, *The Complete Poems and Plays* (New York: Harcourt, Brace & Co., 1952), 136.

5. Seymour Chatman, as quoted in Stephen D. Moore, *Mark and Luke in Poststructuralist Perspectives: Jesus Begins to Write* (New Haven: Yale University Press, 1992), 138.

6. Richard Sennett, *The Uses of Disorder: Personal Identity and City Life* (New York: Knopf, 1970), 96.

7. Bruce Larson, *Living Beyond Our Fears* (New York: Harper & Row, 1990), 123.

8. Freeman Dyson, *From Eros to Gaia* (New York: Pantheon, 1992), 70.

9. William James, "Is Life Worth Living?" *The Will to Believe and Other Essays in Popular Philosophy* (New York: Langmans Green, 1897), 59.

10. "Sickie Awards," *Health,* January-February 1993, 53.

11. Idries Shah, *The Sufis* (Garden City, N.Y.: Doubleday, 1964), 1-10. The quote is on pp. 9-10.

12. As reported in *National & International Religion Report,* 9 January 1995), 6.

13. One of the first assessments of our culture's deep "metaphysical insecurity" was Theodore Roszak's important essay "In Search of the Miraculous," *Harper's,* 262 (January 1981), 54-62. His ending coda calling for "the critical mind open to transcendent energy" (62) is as relevant and moving as the day it was written.

14. See Rowan A. Greer, *The Fear of Freedom: A Study of Miracles in the Roman Imperial Church* (University Park: Pennsylvania State University Press, 1989). The quote is from Everett Ferguson, review of *The Fear of Freedom, Church History* 60 (1961): 94.

15. Rene Latourelle, *The Miracles of Jesus and the Theology of Miracles* (New York: Paulist Press, 1988), 324.

16. Thanks to Barry P. Boulware, for the story from the sermon "When God Prayed to God," originally preached 8 March 1992.

17. David M. Eisenberg and others, "Unconventional Medicine in the United States: Prevalence, Costs, and Patterns of Use," *New England Journal of Medicine* 328 (28 January 1993): 246-52.

18. John Cornwell, *Powers of Darkness, Powers of Light: Travels in Search of the Miraculous and the Demonic* (New York: Penguin, 1992).

19. W. H. Auden, "Concerning the Unpredictable," introduction to Loren Eiseley's *The Star Thrower* (New York: Harcourt, Brace, Jovanovich, 1978), 17.

20. Eliade wrote this in Paris on 23 July 1965. See Eliade, *Journal II, 1957–1969,* trans. by Fred H. Johnson, Jr. (Chicago: University of

Chicago Press, 1989), 267. Originally published as pp. 229 571 of *Fragments d'un journal* (Paris: Editions Gallimard, 1973).
21. Karin Granberg-Michaelson, *Healing Community* (Geneva, Switzerland: WCC Publications, 1991), 14.
22. Latourelle, *The Miracles of Jesus,* 331.

10. Moodle Along the Way

1. John Dominic Crossan, ed. *Sayings Parallels: A Workbook for the Jesus Tradition* (Philadelphia: Fortress Press, 1986), 211.
2. George Eliot, *Middlemarch: A Study of Provincial Life* (New York: Knopf, 1930), 171.
3. As quoted in Gordon MacDonald, *Christ Followers in the Real World* (Nashville: Oliver-Nelson, 1989), 177.
4. Thomas Moore, *Meditations: On the Monk Who Dwells in Daily Life* (San Francisco: HarperSanFrancisco, 1994), 44.
5. Fernando Pessoa, "I Have a Terrible Cold" from *Selected Poems* (New York: Penguin, 1987), 122.
6. Derek Raymond, *The Hidden Files* (London: Little Brown & Co., 1992), 119.
7. Antonio Porchia, *Voices: Aphorisms,* sel. and trans. W. S. Merwin (New York: Knopf, 1988), 32.
8. Bob Benson, *"See You At the House": The Stories Bob Benson Used to Tell* (Nashville: Generoux, 1986), 124.
9. James C. Collins and William C. Lazier, *Beyond Entrepreneurship* (Englewood Cliffs, N.J.: Prentice Hall, 1992), 216.
10. Thomas H. Green, *When the Well Runs Dry* (Notre Dame, Ind.: Ave Maria Press, 1979), 143. For a fuller development of this metaphor of floating, see Green's chapter "To Know the Place for the First Time," 142-65.
11. See John Ashbery's "More Pleasant Adventures" in Ashbery, *A Wave* (New York: Viking Press, 1984), 16.
12. As quoted in Joetta Handrich Schlabach, *Extending the Table: A World Community Cookbook* (Scottdale, Pa.: Herald Press, 1991), 47.